ONESTANDING

North Carolina: 2009 NCAA Champions

Acknowledgments

ONE STANDING: North Carolina 2009 NCAA Champions

PUBLISHERS: Orage Quarles III, The News & Observer, and Ann Caulkins, The Charlotte Observer

EDITORS: Lorenzo Perez and Steve Ruinsky

WRITERS: Robbi Pickeral, Ken Tysiac, Caulton Tudor, A.J. Carr, Scott Fowler, Luciana Chavez

PHOTOGRAPHERS: Robert Willett, Chuck Liddy, Ethan Hyman, Jason Arthurs, Takaaki Iwabu and Shawn Rocco

GRAPHICS AND SPORTS PAGE DESIGN: Jessaca Giglio, Jennifer Bowles, Jon Blasco, Steve Allen

BOOK DESIGN: Chris Fenison, Pediment Publishing

ASSISTANCE IN EDITING: Brooke Cain and Felicia Gressette

ASSISTANCE IN DESIGN AND PHOTOS: Scott Sharpe

EXECUTIVE EDITORS: John Drescher, The News & Observer, and Rick Thames, The Charlotte Observer

Foreword

The North Carolina Tar Heels are college basketball's national champions. That's five NCAA titles for the program and two for head coach Roy Williams, in case you're counting.

Many predicted they'd go all the way, but few could foresee how hard it would be to get there. This veteran team had one goal — to win a championship — and nothing could stand in their way.

High expectations did not scare them.

Injuries to Tyler Hansbrough, Ty Lawson and Marcus Ginyard did not derail them.

The toughest teams in the nation could not stop them.

The Heels' quest started with a loss. Kansas, Williams' old team, pounded UNC in last season's Final Four semifinals. It was a devastating end to what was supposed to be a championship season.

But it motivated Williams' team. Hansbrough, last season's player of the year, decided to come back for his senior year to take another shot at a title. Lawson, Wayne Ellington and Danny Green also returned, forsaking the NBA for a chance to win it all.

The Tar Heels were immediately seen as the team to beat. But there would be bumps along the way.

Hansbrough, the team's best scorer, started the season with a badly injured shin. Ginyard, the team's best defender, missed most of the season with a broken foot. Lawson, the team's best playmaker, was slowed down the stretch by a jammed big toe.

The Tar Heels lost to Boston College in early January, the first of four defeats. They fell from the No. 1 spot in the national rankings, supplanted at times by rivals Duke and Wake Forest.

None of it mattered in the end. North Carolina was playing for one thing, the championship.

Hansbrough returned and broke the all-time ACC scoring record. Lawson persevered and became ACC player of the year. Buoyed by the shooting of Green and Ellington, the Tar Heels powered through the NCAA Tournament, beating a storybook Michigan State team in the championship game

From the hopeful start to the joyful end, the sports staff of The News & Observer and Charlotte Observer was there to tell the story of this remarkable team. Our sportswriters, columnists and photographers — some of the best in the business — followed the Tar Heels from Chapel Hill to Maui, from Greensboro to Detroit, and covered every game of a most memorable season.

Read the stories, enjoy the photographs and savor again North Carolina's championship season.

Table of Contents

A Strong Start: First Half of the Season

November 15, 2008 - January 11, 2009

UNC claims opener; Williams: Heels were a little tight

North Carolina vs. Pennsylvania // W 86-71   November 15, 2008

CHAPEL HILL — North Carolina coach Roy Williams praised his top-ranked Tar Heels some while evaluating their 86-71 season-opening victory over Penn at the Smith Center on Saturday.

He refused to go overboard.

"It was a nice 'W' the first day," Williams said. "We were a little more tight than I wanted to be.

Early in the game, I thought every shot was a good one. We just didn't make many of them."

The Tar Heels (1-0) know victories and respect don't just fall to the No. 1 team in the country.

The best teams also have to work through bad stuff.

Against Penn, which was picked to finish second in the Ivy League, the Heels had to continue figuring out how they would play without injured star Tyler Hansbrough.

And they had to keep on moving while shooting 9-for-27 in the second half.

And freshmen big men Tyler Zeller and Ed Davis had to fight nerves playing their first real game at home.

The Tar Heels made progress on the first front as power forward Deon Thompson scored 17 points with seven rebounds while five others scored at least 10.

Williams praised Thompson for the work he put in during the pre-season, then he nit-picked.

"I think [Thompson] played all right but I don't like the shot he took there at the end," Williams said of a missed 17-footer. "He said his guy fouled him. I said, 'Then you're both not very bright because you're taking a bad shot and he's fouling a bad shot.' ... I thought Deon did some nice things."

The Tar Heels did OK with that last mission as Zeller started the first game of his college career and threw in 18 points. Davis grabbed 14 rebounds with 10 points to finish with his first career double-double.

Davis turned up his intensity two or three days ago.

"I felt like he got every rebound and he dunked everything," UNC junior guard Wayne Ellington said. "I feel like that's what we need. I think we need the high post presence to step up and he's been doing a great job of that."

Williams still wasn't sending candy and roses.

"I love the way Ed and Tyler got involved in the game," Williams said. "I look down and see that Ed had 14 rebounds and that's really good, but I think it's also important for him to not have zero assists and four turnovers. I look down

there and see Tyler is 5-for-8 with 18 points but I don't expect him to have zero defensive rebounds.

"We have to get more consistent play out of them."

Williams said the Tar Heels are a much better shooting team than they showed on Saturday while shooting 28-for-60 in the game (46.7 percent) and 9-for-27 in the second half (33.3 percent).

Ellington, the team's best shooter, was 5-for-15 but scored 13 with five assists and two steals.

The Heels led by 15 at halftime and won the game by 15. They couldn't quite bring the hammer down on the Quakers, who spread the Heels out with zone defense and drained 11 of 33 3-pointers they took.

The Heels' lead oscillated between 10 and 20 points. Penn guard Tyler Bernardini made a 3 — he led all scorers with 26 — with 5:10 left in the game to make it 76-63 Carolina.

UNC guard Ty Lawson turned it over and Penn missed a shot but it got the ball back when Penn forward Jack Eggleston stole the ball

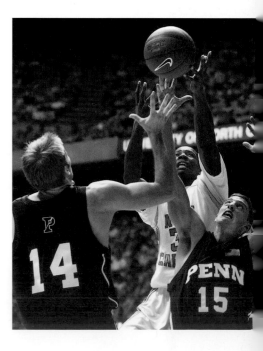

from UNC guard Bobby Frasor before draining a 3 to cut the lead to 10 with 4:02 left in the game.

Zeller made a free throw and Penn's Harrison Gaines missed a jumper that would have cut the lead to nine.

Carolina senior Danny Green, who scored 12 points with four rebounds four assists and three steals, agreed that the Heels were OK with looking a little raw while figure some things out against Penn.

"I think we did OK," Green said. "We had some mental lapses. We can't do that against a really good team because they'll capitalize. Penn is a good team and they came back like any good team.

"[ACC teams] will definitely come back. We'll probably be in the locker room holding our heads wishing we did something because they'll take advantage of it." ∎

— Luciana Chavez

LEFT: North Carolina forward Tyler Zeller (44) scores two of his game-high 18 points on this dunk during the second half. CHUCK LIDDY/THE NEWS & OBSERVER

OPPOSITE LEFT: North Carolina guard Wayne Ellington (22) brings the ball upcourt during the second half. CHUCK LIDDY/THE NEWS & OBSERVER

OPPOSITE RIGHT: North Carolina forward Ed Davis (32) shoots over Pennsylvania's Larry Loughery (14) and Pennsylvania guard Kevin Egee (15) during the second half. CHUCK LIDDY/THE NEWS & OBSERVER

PREVIOUS: UNC's Deon Thompson (21) gets a first half dunk for two of his 22 points in the Tar Heels' 100-84 victory over Oral Roberts in December. ROBERT WILLETT/THE NEWS & OBSERVER

Kentucky can't keep up with talented Heels

North Carolina vs. Kentucky // W 77-58   November 18, 2008

CHAPEL HILL — North Carolina basketball needed a little pick-me-up.

Kentucky supplied it.

The Tar Heels' 77-58 whipping of Kentucky Tuesday night contained basically no drama but bulged with YouTube-worthy plays executed by those in baby blue.

It was 25-6, North Carolina, within the first 8 minutes and the Tar Heels never led by less than 11 after that. That left ESPN with a lot of time to pretend Kentucky could come back and Tar Heels fans with a couple of hours to enjoy themselves in a stress-free environment.

That was significant, because despite being ranked the No. 1 team in the nation, the Tar Heels have experienced some angst lately. Most notably, there is the iffiness of Tyler Hansbrough's right shin.

The shin has kept the formerly indestructible Hansbrough out of the first two games with a "stress reaction" that boomeranged into a stressed-out reaction among the Tar Heel faithful. Then there was UNC's opener Saturday, in which the Tar Heels beat Penn by 15 points — a win that was solid but not overly impressive.

So a blowout of a team with a big name was exactly what the Tar Heels needed and exactly what they got.

Now, Kentucky (0-2) isn't very good these days. Davidson would have been more competition. Shoot, VMI would have been more competition.

Tar Heels coach Roy Williams told the North Carolina students to stop a "V-M-I" chant early in the game, a taunt that referred to Kentucky's season-opening loss to the Keydets. Williams was obviously trying not to embarrass Kentucky's players — but that happened anyway within the first five minutes.

The Wildcats play in Rupp Arena, a 23,000-seat cavern that's a little larger than the Smith Center. Kentucky leads all NCAA Division I schools in total victories (North Carolina is No. 2). So you would think the Wildcats would understand how to start a game in a hostile environment.

They didn't.

The Wildcats committed 17 turnovers in the first half and 28 overall. In the first five minutes particularly, the way Kentucky played was an embarrassment to that school's rich basketball tradition.

Part of that had to do with

WEDNESDAY, NOVEMBER 19, 2008

THE NEWS & OBSERVER

Sports
www.newsobserver.com/sports

SWANK COULD PLAY
Wake Forest's record-setting place-kicker Sam Swank has recovered from injury. **PAGE 5C**

< PEDROIA HONORED
Boston Red Sox second baseman Dustin Pedroia voted AL MVP. **PAGE 8C**

HURRICANES 2
CANADIENS 1

Hurricanes rally to beat Canadiens

Carolina's Samsonov scores his first goal of the season

By CHIP ALEXANDER
STAFF WRITER

RALEIGH – Ray Whitney had the winning goal and Sergei Samsonov scored his first goal of the season. For the Carolina Hurricanes, those were the big talking points Tuesday night after a 2-1 victory over the Montreal Canadiens.

The Canes, trailing 1-0 after two periods, tied the score on Samsonov's shot from the slot at 3:06 of the third, then took the lead on Whitney's power-play goal at 6:33. *Bet close* games more often than not are decided on close plays.

For the Hurricanes and the Canadiens, one came just after Whitney's score. Montreal's Andrei Kostitsyn powered a shot that hit the post, and the puck settled near the goal line before Canes goalie Cam Ward.

Ward, sharp in goal all night, had his eye on the puck. But defenseman Dennis Seidenberg alertly swept in to collect it and clear it out.

"They've got some skilled guys and [Kostitsyn] made something out of nothing and put a good shot on the post," Ward said. "I'd like to think I was in good position, and I turned my head and 'Seids' [Seidenberg] was already there, so there was no panic.

"We were able to get it out and act like nothing happened."

When Carolina was losing three in a row and four of five, what everything bad seemed to happen to the Canes, the puck might have bounced toward the net

SEE HURRICANES, PAGE 6C

Carolina's Ray Whitney celebrates after scoring the eventual game-winning goal.
STAFF PHOTO BY CHRIS SEWARD

'Just another game' a boost for Samsonov

RALEIGH — The morning of the 19th game of the season, with Sergei Samsonov still looking for his first goal, he was asked if Tuesday night's opponent might not shake something loose.

After all, the slumping Carolina Hurricanes forward was run out of Montreal in the summer of 2007 after a dismal season for the Canadiens, only to resurrect his career last spring with the Canes.

"It's just another game," Samsonov said, shaking his head. Maybe. Maybe not.

Luke
DeCock

Early in the third period, with the Canes down a goal, Samsonov took a pass from Patrick Eaves on the rush, cut to the middle and slipped a shot past Carey Price to send the Canes on their way to a 2-1 win.

It was a big goal, but sometimes, the gap between zero and (1), as in "Samsonov (1)," is the biggest of all.

"It's a bit of a relief, you know?" Samsonov said. "Any time you're in a slump, it's a confidence thing more than anything. You get chances, and it's frustrating when they don't go in, so it was nice to see that one go in."

Samsonov's goal defibrillated the RBC Center and

SEE DECOCK, PAGE 6C

NORTH CAROLINA 77, KENTUCKY 58

Heels win and worry

ALREADY WITHOUT HANSBROUGH, UNC FACES LOSING ZELLER, TOO

By ROBBIE PICKERAL
STAFF WRITER

CHAPEL HILL – North Carolina blew out Kentucky 77-58 with one Tyler sitting on the bench in street clothes Tuesday night.

Now, the top-ranked Tar Heels might have to worry about playing without another.

With 1:26 left, freshman Tyler Zeller — who started his second straight basketball game in place of All-America Tyler Hansbrough, who is still resting a "stress reaction" to his right shin — injured his left wrist on a missed breakaway dunk.

He was fouled in transition by Wildcats forward Ramon Harris, came down hard on his left hand, eventually walked off the court alongside a trainer and was taken to a hospital for tests.

"It doesn't look good; it doesn't give us a good feeling right now," UNC coach Roy Williams said.

Asked for more clarification, Williams said: "I'm not a doctor ... but when I'm over there with him, he really felt a lot of pain. It was right on his wrist ... he came down, that's the first thing that hit the floor.

"And let's get something straight: I think it was an aggressive play by their youngster [Harris] — he was trying to block the shot. It was a hard foul, but I don't think it was a dirty foul."

A team spokesman said there would not be an update on Zeller's health until today at the earliest.

With starting forward Marcus Ginyard also still sidelined after foot surgery, Zeller's injury cast a pall on what was an otherwise dominating game by the Tar Heels (2-0), who got a career-high 20 points from junior Deon Thompson and beat the Wildcats (0-2) for the fifth straight time.

UNC commanded so overwhelmingly from the outset that Williams had to shush the student section from chanting "VMI! VMI!" — the team that upset Kentucky in the Wildcats' season-opener — barely 5½ minutes into the game.

The big reason for Carolina's early onslaught was Thompson, who did most of his damage in the first half.

He had six points, four rebounds and a block in the opening

SEE UNC, PAGE 4C

FIRST LOOK
PLENTY OF ACTION FROM CHAPEL HILL

See more photos and a first edit of the photographers' images from Tuesday's game, plus video of the play on which UNC's Tyler Zeller was injured.

newsobserver.com

Going for a block, Kentucky's Ramon Harris fouls UNC's Tyler Zeller on a second-half play that ends with Zeller hitting the floor and injuring his left wrist. The Tar Heels await a report on Zeller's status today.
STAFF PHOTO BY ROBERT WILLETT

Kentucky can't keep up with talented Heels

CHAPEL HILL – North Carolina basketball needed a little pick-me-up. Kentucky supplied it.

The Tar Heels' 77-58 whipping of Kentucky Tuesday night contained basically no drama but bulged with YouTube-worthy plays executed by those in baby blue.

It was 25-6, North Carolina, within the first 8 minutes and exactly what the

Scott Fowler

Tar Heels never led by less than 11 after that. That left ESPN with a lot of time to pretend Kentucky could come back and Tar Heels fans with a couple of hours to enjoy themselves in a stress-free environment.

That was significant, because despite being ranked the No. 1 team in the nation, the Tar Heels have experienced some angst lately. Most notably, there is the illness of Tyler Hansbrough's right shin.

The shin has kept the formerly indestructible Hansbrough out of the first two games with a "stress reaction" that boomeranged into a stressed-out reaction among the Tar Heel faithful. Then there was UNC's opener Saturday, in which the Tar Heels beat Penn by 15 points — a win that was solid but not overly impressive.

So a blowout of a team with a big name was exactly what the Tar Heels needed and exactly what they got.

Now, Kentucky (0-2) isn't very good these days. Davidson would have been more competition. Shoot, VMI would have been more competition.

Tar Heels coach Roy Williams told the North Carolina students to stop a "VMI!" chant early in the game, a taunt that referred to Kentucky's season-opening loss to the Keydets. Williams was obviously trying not to embarrass Kentucky's players — but that happened anyway within

SEE FOWLER, PAGE 4C

Kentucky coach Billy Gillispie exhorts his overmatched Wildcats, who are struggling to find their way this season.
STAFF PHOTO BY ROBERT WILLETT

North Carolina's excellent defense. Williams said he thought his team had a "fantastic first 10-12 minutes." Then, he said, the Tar Heels "meandered around." But that's ol' Roy — he wants perfection.

On the offensive end, Tar Heel junior forward Deon Thompson (20 points, nine rebounds) had the game of his life. Thompson, who has a tendency to fade out of games, looked like he was channeling Hansbrough's intensity all night before fouling out late and receiving a standing ovation. Thompson later said the relatively easy win demonstrated "how deep we really are."

The only minor chord struck in this one for North Carolina was a late injury to freshman center Tyler Zeller. Zeller hurt his left wrist after getting fouled on a dunk attempt in transition, and Williams was concerned after the game that Zeller might have broken the wrist and be out for awhile.

Williams also said afterward,

however, that Hansbrough could have already played if the Tar Heels really had needed him to. So it may be that the young Tyler is about to exit for awhile, but the All-American Tyler is close to checking back in.

In any event, these Tar Heels are obviously deep enough to shrug off one or two major injuries.

All things are possible for this North Carolina squad.

On Tuesday night, they reminded us of that. ∎

— Scott Fowler

ABOVE: Kentucky fan and actress Ashley Judd stands in the UNC student section during the North Carolina vs. Kentucky game. ROBERT WILLETT/THE NEWS & OBSERVER

OPPOSITE: UNC's Ed Davis (32) defends the basket against Kentucky's Jodie Meeks (23) in the first half. ROBERT WILLETT/THE NEWS & OBSERVER

Green powers Heels; With Tyler Hansbrough and Tyler Zeller out of the lineup, Danny Green steps up

North Carolina vs. Chaminade // W 115-70   November 24, 2008

LAHAINA, Hawaii — Even down four players, top-ranked North Carolina was too much — and too many — for its first-round Maui Invitational foe.

When point guard Ty Lawson wasn't racing past undermanned Chaminade, forward Danny Green was dunking over the Silverswords at Lahaina Civic Center on Monday night. The result: a 115-70 blowout that marked the most points UNC has ever scored in this tournament. Green chipped in 26 of those, a career high.

The victory bumped UNC's record to 11-2 all time in the tournament; it will play the winner of the Alabama-Oregon game.

"I felt for Matt [Mahar, Chaminade's coach], to only have seven guys to play against a team like us, that loves to go up and down the court," UNC coach Roy Williams said. "I think stamina was a big issue."

Which was saying something, because UNC didn't have its full allotment of players, either.

All-American Tyler Hansbrough, who made his season debut Friday at UC Santa Barbara after resting a stress reaction in his right shin for more than three weeks, was in uniform but did not start, joining Tyler Zeller (out for the season with a broken wrist), Marcus Ginyard (foot surgery) and Mike Copeland (knee surgery) on the casually attired bench.

The move to sit the senior wasn't surprising, considering Williams had expressed concern at the idea of playing Hansbrough in every contest of the three-games-in-three-days tournament.

Williams also said Hansbrough is questionable for tonight.

"I think if it had been for a national championship, he would have played. But I made a decision before we left Santa Barbara that I was not going to play him three straight games," Williams said. "He tweaked his ankle a little bit against Santa Barbara; that's the problem right now, it's not even his shin, so I have no idea if he's going to play tomorrow night. I did not plan for him to sit out two games, so if he does sit out, it would be because of his ankle, not his shin."

Freshman Ed Davis (nine points, eight rebounds) made his first collegiate start in Hansbrough's place, and the lesser number of bodies made for some creative lineups, which also included sliding Bobby Frasor to small forward and Green to power forward once in a while.

It also made for a stilted half-court attack in the beginning — until Lawson took control, and UNC scored point after point in transition.

Chaminade scored the opening points at Lahaina Civic Center, but UNC pulled away for good when it held the Silverswords to two field goals in the final eight minutes of the first half.

The Silverswords — a Division II team that serves as host of the Invitational — simply had no answer for Lawson, or UNC's runaway style.

Lawson fed Green an alley-oop then scored five straight points in the final 1:32 before halftime. Lawson had 14 points and three assists by that point, and UNC had a comfy 48-25 lead.

"I was just getting in the passing lanes, trying to get my hand on the ball ... just looking for my shot," said Lawson, who finished with 19 points, six assists and zero turnovers.

Lawson opened the second half with a 3-pointer and a layup for the Tar Heels, who rotated in their nine healthy scholarship players in order to balance the minutes, and potential wear that could come from playing so many games in a row.

Then Green, who had eight points in the first half, took over, and outscored Chaminade 11-2 all by himself to give his team an 83-39 lead with 10:24 left.

"I just ran the floor, got some easy baskets — and a lot of good passes from Ty," Green said.

He went to the bench shortly after that, and Williams started inserting the walk-ons with 5:44 left.

Green added six rebounds, four assists and a block to his career-best day.

Shane Hanson led Chaminade with 15 points. ∎

— Robbi Pickeral

Heels blow past Ducks; Hansbrough, Green set tone

North Carolina vs. Oregon // W 98-69   November 25, 2008

LAHAINA, Hawaii — The two North Carolina teams to win the Maui Invitational have gone on to advance to the Final Four. With Tyler Hansbrough back in the lineup, it appears the top-ranked Tar Heels could repeat the feat.

Technically, Carolina didn't need Hansbrough's 16 points or four rebounds to blow out Oregon 98-69 in the eight-team tournament's semifinals Tuesday night at Lahaina Civic Center.

Not with senior forward Danny Green setting a career high for 3-pointers (five) in the first half, and freshman Ed Davis coming off the bench to record the second double-double of his career.

But the senior All-American added some needed depth in the lane and that special brand of "Psycho T" aggressiveness that was missing when he sat out three of UNC's first four games because of a stress reaction in his right shin, then a "tweaked" left ankle.

And now that he's warmed up, his presence will be particularly important tonight, when the Tar Heels (5-0) play No. 8 Notre Dame — which survived a last-second comeback attempt by seventh-ranked Texas in the other semifinal game — at 10 (EST) in the tournament final.

Hansbrough, the reigning national player of the year, will likely match up against 6-foot-8 Irish forward Luke Harangody, the reigning Big East player of the year.

If Hansbrough plays, that is.

"Any decision on whether Tyler plays tomorrow night will be made during warm-ups," UNC coach Roy Williams said. "... If he has any pain in his ankle, we probably won't play him; if he doesn't, we probably will play him."

Hansbrough scored UNC's first points against the Ducks (3-2), tipping in a shot to tie it 2-2. UNC never trailed after that.

By halftime, the forward was so tenacious that had passed seven players on the NCAA list for attempted free throws; he made 8 of 10 attempts and was ranked 11th on the list at the break and after the game.

"I feel good; it feels good to get back out there and get in the groove of things," Hansbrough said. "Conditioning, I'm a little out of shape. But that will come, the more I play, the more I practice. My ankle, I felt it a little bit, but overall, I felt pretty good."

Getting to the line was just part of Carolina's early domination.

After Oregon's Tajuan Porter made a 3-pointer to cut his team's deficit to 18-11 with about 13 minutes left in the first half, UNC sprinted on a 17-1 run during which Green buried one of his five first-half 3-pointers and the Ducks missed everything from outside shots to tips.

Davis, meanwhile, was trying to grab every missed shot in sight — and he got a lot of them. He had seven rebounds by the half, and Green had 15 points, all on 3-pointers. His previous high from behind the arc was four.

The Tar Heels, who harassed Oregon into 21.1-percent shooting in the first 20 minutes, led 51-22 at halftime and never let up.

UNC took a 30-point lead when Wayne Ellington buried a 3-pointer for the Heels' first bucket of the second half.

And despite some sloppiness that had Williams' scream "Hey! Play smarter than that," there was no reason to worry about a serious Oregon comeback.

Hansbrough was pulled with 11:56 left, after he buried two more free throws. In the end, he made 2 of 4 field goals and was 12-for-14 from the line.

Green, who scored a career-high 26 points against Chaminade on Monday, finished with 21 points and eight rebounds. He has now recorded the two best two-scoring days of his career in this tournament.

"It's just my teammates finding me when I'm open; there's no real big secret to it," Green said. "[Opponents] focus so much on Tyler on the inside, and Ty [Lawson] when he's penetrating, and Wayne. We have so many threats that it just leaves me open sometimes. I'm lucky enough to be open at the right spot at the right time, and they found me and I knocked a couple in." ∎

— Robbi Pickeral

ABOVE: Down by 50 points in the second half to the Tar Heels, UNC Asheville head coach Eddie Biedenbach (center) and his assistants show signs of disappointment after a long night on Sunday, November 30, 2008.
ROBERT WILLETT/THE NEWS & OBSERVER

Heels race by Irish; Tyler Hansbrough erupts for 34 points and Ty Lawson's speed overwhelms Notre Dame

North Carolina vs. ⁸Notre Dame // W 102-87   November 26, 2008

LAHAINA, Hawaii — With about 10 minutes left Wednesday night, North Carolina point guard Ty Lawson assisted big man Tyler Hansbrough on a racing, rousing breakaway dunk.

It was just like old times — and with a championship attached.

A healthy Hansbrough and invigorated Lawson combined to lead the top-ranked Tar Heels to a dominating 102-87 victory over No. 8 Notre Dame for the Maui Invitational title.

Considering the fact that UNC went on to the NCAA Final Four after the previous two times they won a first-place trophy at Lahaina Civic Center, the Tar Heels hope it's just the first such celebration of the season.

Playing in just his third game of the season after sitting out more than three weeks because of a stress reaction in his right shin, Hansbrough finished with 34 points, five rebounds and two blocked shots.

Lawson, so fast with the ball that the Fighting Irish might remember him only as a blur, chipped in 22 points and 11 assists in earning tournament MVP honors.

It was apparent early why Carolina coach Roy Williams had been so cautious with Hansbrough's playing time in the past few weeks — because the senior All-American forward was anything but cautious from the outset.

The lead swapped back and forth

early, with Notre Dame big man Luke Harangody (13 points, eight rebounds) trying to establish himself in the lane and Hansbrough trying to establish himself everywhere.

UNC's big man scored 10 points in the first 10 minutes.

Then, with about 8:30 left in the

ABOVE: UNC's Wayne Ellington (22) and head coach Roy Williams react after Danny Green hits his sixth three-point shot in the second half. Green scored 18 points in the game. ROBERT WILLETT/THE NEWS & OBSERVER

OPPOSITE: UNC's Ty Lawson (5) traps UNC Asheville's J.P. Primm (10) during the first half. ROBERT WILLETT/THE NEWS & OBSERVER

first half and UNC holding a 28-25 lead, Lawson fueled a 12-2 run that included five points from the junior point guard, a baseline jumper from Hansbrough and a couple of steals and dunks from forward Deon Thompson.

Carolina led by as many as 13 points before the break, when Hansbrough buried just the fourth 3-pointer of his career to make it 46-33.

The Tar Heels didn't quite manage to hold the Irish under 30 percent shooting in the first half, as it had done with their previous two tournament foes. But it was close, as Notre Dame shot just 35.9 percent.

Notre Dame tried to rally in the closing minutes, with guard Kyle McAlarney (39 points) burying 3-pointer after 3-pointer to try to keep the Irish's hope alive. But they couldn't quite counter Hansbrough's power or Lawson's speed.

Thompson added 19 points and 12 rebounds for UNC, which is now 13-2 all time in the Maui Invitational. ∎

— Robbi Pickeral

Green sparks barrage

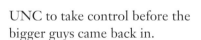
North Carolina vs. UNC-Asheville // W 116-48   November 30, 2008

CHAPEL HILL — The highlight of this matchup the past couple of seasons had been counting how many dunks 7-foot-7 UNC-Asheville center Kenny George could slam without leaving the floor.

With the big man sidelined during the top-ranked Tar Heels' 116-48 blowout Sunday night, the fun part for North Carolina fans was following how many 3-pointers Danny Green could swish before he finally missed.

The answer was six — all in the second half — which accounted for all 18 of the senior's points and a good portion of UNC's season-high 27 3-point attempts.

"At the end, the last couple were mostly heat-checks — to see if I could make it, or how close I could come," Green said of his 3-point barrage. "We were just having fun."

It was that kind of game for the Tar Heels, who remained unbeaten (7-0) by scoring the most points in coach Roy Williams' six-year tenure as head coach. The blowout marked the Tar Heels' largest margin of victory under Williams and the third-largest winning margin in school history.

"We just made a bunch of shots, and they missed a bunch of shots, and that was the ballgame," Williams said.

With UNC All-American Tyler Hansbrough sitting out his fourth game of the season, this time because of a sore left ankle, and George at home in Chicago still recovering after having part of his right foot amputated as a result of an antibiotic-resistant staph infection, the Bulldogs opened the game with a 6-2 lead.

That prompted Williams to pull starting forwards Deon Thompson and Ed Davis off the floor "because I didn't think they were very focused at all."

The result was the smallest lineup in recent Tar Heels history — the 6-6 Green at center, 6-6 Will Graves at power forward and 6-3 Bobby Frasor at wing forward. But it led to a 13-1 run that allowed UNC to take control before the bigger guys came back in.

Point guard Ty Lawson dominated throughout and scored 14 of his team-high 22 points by halftime, when UNC led 53-19.

Then Green, who had previously topped his career high for 3-pointers in the Maui Invitational last week, went to work. He hit his first shot from behind the arc 27 seconds into the second half to make the score 56-19.

His third, with 16:35 left, gave the Tar Heels a 40-point lead.

And his sixth, which he shot while standing on the outline of the state of North-Carolina sticker at midcourt, made it 82-32.

"You start to test yourself — where can I shoot it from and make it?" Green said.

"... I heard, 'THREE!' [from the crowd], and I'm like, 'I'm not shooting this.' But nobody stopped the ball. So why not?"

Green finally was pulled from the game by Williams about a minute later, after his second shot from near the sticker missed.

But the tone was set. Lawson made two of four 3-point attempts for the game, and walk-on J.B. Tanner came off the bench in the final minutes to add two swishes from behind the arc, as well.

UNC's 14 made 3-pointers were the most since it also hit 14 against Virginia in January 2005. And in such a lopsided blowout, it gave the fans something to watch.

"Danny got us all excited, and got everybody riled up, and we were just happy," guard Wayne Ellington said. "I thought it was contagious; everybody started knocking down shots after that." ∎

— Robbi Pickeral

Tar Heels dismantle Spartans; Lawson, Hansbrough lead the way for UNC

North Carolina vs. [13]Michigan State // W 98-63   December 3, 2008

DETROIT — If North Carolina wants to return here in April, it needs to keep playing like this.

Ty Lawson sped, Tyler Hansbrough dominated and UNC rolled to a 98-63 blowout win over No. 13 Michigan State in the ACC-Big Ten Challenge.

The top-ranked Tar Heels (8-0) have now won five of their past six games in the made-for-ESPN event.

But more important to their quest to return to Ford Field for the Final Four, they have now beaten two top-15 teams in the last eight days.

"It's pretty impressive, this team, having a schedule like that — eight games in 18 days, Coach [Roy] Williams told us," guard Bobby Frasor said after the Tar Heels held the Spartans to 20-percent shooting in the second half. "And we're even banged up, [so] to play the way that we did is pretty impressive.

"We can still get better — I don't know if that's scary or what for other teams, but we have a chance to be a really, really good team."

Although the Tar Heels will eventually be tested, they made things look easy again Wednesday night.

Hansbrough, the All-American forward who had missed four of the Tar Heels' first seven games while resting a stress reaction in his right shin, then

LEFT: UNC's Ed Davis (32) gets a second half dunk over UNC Asheville. Davis scored 13 points in the game. ROBERT WILLETT/THE NEWS & OBSERVER

BELOW: UNC's Tyler Hansbrough (50) puts up a shot under pressure from Michigan State's Raymar Morgan (2) in the first half. ROBERT WILLETT/ THE NEWS & OBSERVER

a "tweaked" left ankle, started and scored the first six points of the game for North Carolina, which never trailed.

The Spartans, behind forward Raymar Morgan and guard Chris Allen, remained scrappy early, cutting their deficit to 33-29 with about six minutes left in the first half when Allen buried a 3-pointer. But UNC countered with an 11-4 run — during which five different Tar Heels scored — to pull away.

And although MSU shot 51.6 percent in the first half, UNC also shot better than 50 percent for the 10th straight half.

Carolina led 53-39 at the break, but opened the second half with a 14-2 run during which the Spartans made only one field goal, a layup by Morgan, in the first 7:12.

By the time Morgan made another layup to end his team's scoring drought, UNC had already scored 67 points, which was what the Spartans (4-2) had been allowing opponents to average this season.

"The second half, they seemed to lose their legs a little bit," Williams said. "There's no way our defense caused them to shoot 20 percent. I hope that I was substituting, and I hope that I was trying to force the pace and make the teams go up and down the court, and [that] might have had something to do with it also."

Because while the Spartans appeared to grow tired, the Tar Heels kept coming — in waves.

Hansbrough looked healthy as ever, mixing in jumpers with power moves. His 11 rebounds were a season-high, and he also scored 25 points, leaving him 35 short of Phil Ford's career scoring record at UNC.

Lawson, who always enjoys match-ups against other speedsters, such as MSU's Kalin Lucas, didn't look overly winded after showing off his improved outside game and finishing with 17 points and eight assists. He now has dished out 38 assists with only three turnovers over his last five games.

And wing guard Wayne Ellington, who had become almost an after-thought early this season, what with Hansbrough's injury, Deon Thompson's aggressiveness, Lawson's speed and Danny Green's 3-point shooting, again showed why he is such a valuable asset. He scored 13 of his 17 points in the first half.

Morgan led Michigan State with 21 points.

And the Tar Heels left with the goal of a return trip.

"At halftime, Coach Williams told us, 'Twenty more minutes; let's finish this out, and hopefully, if we get a chance, we can be back here in a couple of months,' " Frasor said. "We know what's at stake. ... We all want to come back here. I was thinking about how different it will look — blue carpet with the Final Four, and the NCAA putting up signs as to which team locker room we would be in. It will look a lot different in April." ■

— Robbi Pickeral

LEFT: Michigan State head coach Tom Izzo watches his team fall behind early in the first half against North Carolina. ROBERT WILLETT/THE NEWS & OBSERVER

BELOW: UNC's Ty Lawson (5) leads a fast break in the second half. ROBERT WILLETT/THE NEWS & OBSERVER

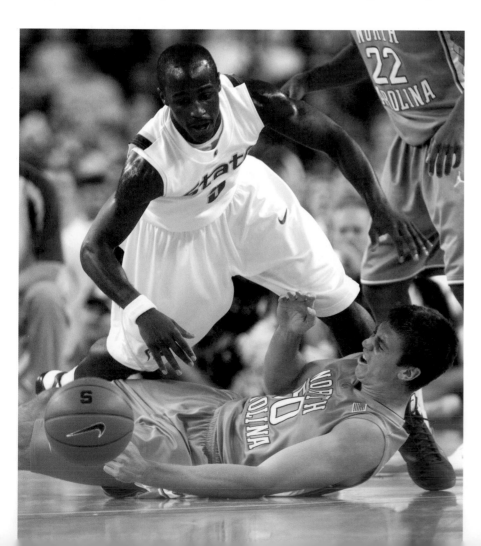

Heels shake off rust; Tyler Hansbrough scores 26, nine shy of a new UNC career scoring mark

| North Carolina vs. Oral Roberts // W 100-84 | December 13, 2008 |

CHAPEL HILL — When North Carolina forward Tyler Hansbrough hit his first five shots Saturday night, teammate Bobby Frasor figured the senior might go ahead and surpass Phil Ford's three-decades-old career record for points.

As it is, Hansbrough now needs only five more field goals — at most — to do it.

Playing in his first home game of the season, the All-American scored 26 points and pulled down nine rebounds in the Tar Heels' 100-84 victory over Oral Roberts — all with a cut on his left knee that required two stitches after the game.

That leaves him nine points away from breaking Ford's school mark of 2,290 points, set in 1978. He'll likely move atop the list Thursday against Evansville.

"It's hard not to think about it," Hansbrough said of the looming record, "but I wasn't thinking about, 'How many points away am I?' or anything like that.

"It is a big deal to me, but I think it will mean more to me when the season's over, and I can look back. I'm more concentrating on this year, as a team thing."

As far as the "team thing," against Oral Roberts (2-7), UNC coach Roy Williams said the top-ranked Tar Heels' performance "was probably the least efficient we have been all year."

The 10-day, final-exam break helps explains a bit why Carolina (9-0) was outrebounded by seven, outscored by four in the second half

and allowed a 24-point lead to be whittled to as little as 14 with about 10 minutes left.

"We were not sharp at all; we were not very good defensively at all," said Williams, who plans to practice the kinks out of his players early this week.

UNC was never really in jeopardy, though, particularly because of the play of Hansbrough, who had sat out four games this season (including three at home) because of injuries to his shin and ankle.

He said his conditioning still leaves a lot to be desired, but it didn't look it as he walked onto the court, needing 35 points to break Ford's record.

The big man didn't even attempt a shot during his first 3 1/2-minute stretch, but after going to the bench to have his left knee bandaged because of a superficial cut sustained when he ran into the broadcast table, he checked back in and scored nine points in a 1:49 span.

That gave the Tar Heels a 27-14 advantage, and the Golden Eagles (2-7) never really stood a chance after that.

"When he started off, hitting 5-for-5, I thought he might go for 35 tonight," Frasor said.

And he might have, Williams said, if he had made more than nine of his 18 shots.

As it was, he scored in familiar Hansbrough fashion — putbacks and free throws — and continued to showcase his extended range via jump shots and a 3-pointer.

And when he wasn't scoring, forward Deon Thompson (career-high 22 points, eight rebounds) and point guard Ty Lawson (18 points, seven assists) took up the slack. Wing Danny Green also chipped in 12

points before he had to leave the game to get five stitches above his right eye.

Robert Jarvis led the Golden Eagles with 26, matching Hansbrough for the game high

---

SUNDAY, DECEMBER 14, 2008   THE NEWS & OBSERVER

A ■ ■ ■ C +

Sports
www.newsobserver.com/sports

BRADFORD WINS HEISMAN
Oklahoma quarterback Sam Bradford beats out Florida QB Tim Tebow and Texas QB Colt McCoy to win college football's biggest award. **PAGE 11C**

N.C. STATE 74 / WSSU 46

Pack cruises to win
McCauley leads way with 14 points

By KEN TYSIAC
STAFF WRITER

RALEIGH — Coach Sidney Lowe had to take his eyes off a defensive possession for the conversation with sophomore point guard Javi Gonzalez.

The point was important enough that Lowe had to make it immediately. In the third minute of the second half of N.C. State's 74-46 defeat of Winston-Salem State on Saturday at Reynolds Coliseum, Lowe removed Gonzalez following a turnover.

Gonzalez had tracked down a long defensive rebound but didn't secure the ball well enough before turning up the court. He lost possession on a held ball in the backcourt.

"He just told me to grab it," Gonzalez said. "I was trying to start the fast break right away, and it didn't work out."

Except for its failure to protect the ball, N.C. State (5-1) bounced back nicely from the previous week's loss to Davidson in Charlotte. Center Ben McCauley led the way with 14 points and nine rebounds, barely missing a fourth straight double-double.

Even though forward Courtney Fells and point guard Farnold Degand were watching from the bench, the Wolfpack shot 51.9 percent from the field and held undersized Winston-Salem State to 28.1 percent.

Fells had a bruised ankle and Degand — who had missed three of the previous four games with a knee injury — was suspended by Lowe for an undisclosed violation of team rules. Lowe said he hasn't decided whether Degand will

SEE N.C. STATE, PAGE 9C

NORTH CAROLINA 100, ORAL ROBERTS 84

Thompson gives Hansbrough a hand

UNC's Tyler Hansbrough tries to steal the ball from Oral Roberts' Marcus Lewis during the Tar Heels' 100-84 win.
STAFF PHOTO BY ROBERT WILLETT

N.C. State's Ben McCauley, right, pulls down a rebound at Reynolds Coliseum.
STAFF PHOTO BY ETHAN HYMAN

PHOTO GALLERIES
See more images and a First Look from the game.
newsobserver.com/multimedia

Tyler Hansbrough scores 26, nine shy of setting a new UNC career scoring mark, and Deon Thompson adds 22 for Heels.

By ROBBI PICKERAL
STAFF WRITER

CHAPEL HILL — Forward Tyler Hansbrough did not set North Carolina's career scoring record Saturday night; instead, teammate Deon Thompson recorded a personal best. Hansbrough had 26 points — nine short of surpassing Phil Ford's three-decades-old

PHOTO GALLERIES
See more images and a First Look from the game.
newsobserver.com/multimedia

mark — and Thompson added a career-high 22 points as top-ranked UNC beat Oral Roberts 100-84 at the Smith Center.

After a 10-day break for final exams, the Tar Heels (9-0) were sloppy in stretches. Still, the game hardly seemed like a test. Hansbrough walked onto the court needing 35 points to break Ford's record of 2,290 points. The senior didn't even attempt a shot during his first 3½-minute stretch, but after going to the bench to have his left knee bandaged because of a superficial cut sustained when he ran into the broadcast table, he checked back in and scored nine points in a 1:49 span.

That gave the Tar Heels a 27-14 advantage, and the Golden Eagles (2-7) never really stood a chance after that.

In all, Hansbrough — who has missed four games this season because of shin and ankle injuries — made his first five shots of the game and finished 9-for-18,

SEE UNC, PAGE 9C

FLYERS 6 / PENGUINS 3

Flyers down Penguins
Knuble scores twice for Philly

THE ASSOCIATED PRESS

PHILADELPHIA — Mike Knuble and the Philadelphia Flyers are enjoying playing hockey again.

Knuble scored twice and the Flyers won their fourth straight game with a 6-3 win over the Pittsburgh Penguins on Saturday.

Philadelphia is 12-1-3 in its last 16 games and has secured 27 of a possible 32 points to move into second place in the Atlantic Division behind the New York Rangers.

"It's fun to come in and pick up the paper and see us climbing in the standings," Knuble said. "It's two points that they can't have and two more that we were able to get."

Joffrey Lupul, Mike Richards, Scott Hartnell and Jeff Carter also scored, and Kimmo Timonen added a career-high four assists, as the Flyers extended their unbeaten streak at home in regulation to nine games (7-0-2).

"It was a chance to make a statement game at home and keep the momentum going," Knuble said. Jordan Staal, Eric Godard and

SEE FLYERS, PAGE 6C

LATE GAME
The Hurricanes-Rangers game did not end by press time for this edition of The N&O. For a report, go to: www.newsobserver.com/sports

Tar Heels won't be underdogs

By RACHEL ULLRICH
CORRESPONDENT

FRISCO, Texas — North Carolina coach Elmar Bolowich doesn't believe in the term "underdog." Being an underdog means being submissive, he said, and his team isn't one to give in easily.

Exhibit A — the Tar Heels have fought their way into today's title game of the NCAA College Cup against Maryland. And while it might not be an underdog, the team does have a handy grudge factor to motivate it.

"Yeah, I think we definitely have a chip on our shoulder. We know that we're good, we know that we can compete, and we just have to prove it now," senior midfielder Garry Lewis said. "Coach was talking about it in the locker room — it's about pride, it's about

SEE SOCCER, PAGE 11C

TODAY
WHO: UNC vs. Maryland
WHEN: 1 p.m.
TV: ESPN2

Recruits getting younger and younger
Basketball coaches now offering scholarships to athletes in ninth and 10th grade

By KEN TYSIAC
STAFF WRITER

At 15, Tyler Lewis is used to being the youngest and smallest player on the court.

He's already in his third season starting for a high school varsity basketball team even though he's just a ninth grader and 5 feet 10, 145 pounds.

But he has exceptional passing ability and a dead-on jump shot from 22 feet at Forsyth Country Day. And he already has coaches with the Charlotte 49ers, Auburn and Virginia Tech telling him they will pay his tuition, room and board if he will play basketball for them.

PHOTO GALLERY
To see more images of Tyler Lewis go to: newsobserver.com/multimedia

"At first I thought it was a joke," Tyler said of his first offer, from Virginia Tech, which came last summer.

"It's no joke. College coaches looking for a competitive edge are in some cases recruiting and accepting commitments from players earlier than ever.

Earlier this year, a player committed to Kentucky before picking a high school.

Recruiting analysts say about

10 current sophomores and a couple freshmen have committed to schools for basketball. Some coaches and administrators say it's not wise to put the pressure of choosing a college on teenagers who aren't mature enough to make such a decision.

"Kids aren't rational, autonomous decision makers," said William Morgan, a sports ethics expert at the University of Southern California. "... They seldom think about the long-term consequences of their actions."

The NCAA, the governing body of college sports, doesn't have a rule preventing coaches from offering and securing non-

binding verbal agreements from players of any age. But the National Association of Basketball Coaches' board of directors in June asked coaches not to offer scholarships or accept commitments from players before June 15 following their sophomore year of high school.

Before then, some coaches say, it's difficult to predict a player's athletic and academic potential. The NABC doesn't have power to enforce its principles beyond perhaps withholding Final Four tickets from coaches who don't follow them.

Despite his youth, Tyler Lewis, 15, has already been offered a college scholarship by three major universities.
CHARLOTTE OBSERVER PHOTO BY DEDRA LAIRD

SEE RECRUITS, PAGE 8C

19

"Tonight he had 26 points and nine rebounds, and to think that he didn't play that well," Williams said of his big man. "He has set such a high standard; he is such a consistent performer — night in and night out, every practice and every game."

Which explains why he's only a handful of shots from making history. ■

— Robbi Pickeral

ABOVE: UNC's Deon Thompson (21) makes a steal from Oral Roberts' Andre Hardy (0). ROBERT WILLETT/THE NEWS & OBSERVER

RIGHT: UNC's Danny Green (14) blocks a shot by Oral Roberts' Kevin Ford (34) in the first half. ROBERT WILLETT/THE NEWS & OBSERVER

2,302 and counting; Attention on record-setting UNC senior Tyler Hansbrough

North Carolina vs. Evansville // W 91-73   December 18, 2008

CHAPEL HILL — Since the day he stepped foot on North Carolina's campus, forward Tyler Hansbrough has been working to diversify his offensive resume by trying to extend his shooting range.

But it seemed appropriate that when it came time to break UNC's three-decades-old career scoring record during the top-ranked Tar Heels' 91-73 basketball victory over Evansville on Thursday night, the senior went back to an old staple: a workmanlike power move.

With 7:42 left in the first half at the Smith Center, Hansbrough muscled around Purple Aces forwards James Haarsma and Pieter van Tongeren to bank in a shot off the glass and score his 10th point

of the game and 2,292nd point of his career. That basket broke the mark of 2,290 that point guard Phil Ford set from 1974 to 1978.

Hansbrough finished with 20 points and now has 2,302 for his career.

"It was very fitting — three guys on him, he was moving to the basket, kind of off-balance, he banks it in with his soft hands," said Gene Hansbrough, who surprised his son by attending the game. "It was a perfect shot for Tyler to break the record on."

Point guard Ty Lawson also chipped in 16 points for the Tar Heels (10-0), though coach Roy Williams looked frustrated at times by his team's performance, particularly after Evansville's Shy Ely

ended the first half with a dunk. That led the coach to stomp off the court despite the fact that his team led by 18 points.

The night, however, belonged to Hansbrough, who accepted the game ball and an embrace from Ford, now an assistant coach for the NBA's Charlotte Bobcats, immediately after setting the record.

After the game, Ford pressed his hands together and bowed to the big man at mid-court, congratulating him as fans in the sellout crowd — some of whom held signs reading "Phil Ford 2,290" on one side and "Tyler 2,291+" on the other — were on their feet for a rousing ovation.

"It's an honor to be compared in the same breath at Tyler," Ford said later. "When I see how hard he plays, and how he listens to Coach Williams — as a player, that's why I tried to do."

Then Hansbrough — who followed his record-breaking bucket with a missed dunk attempt that probably will make the team blooper reel — choked up as he watched a montage of current and

former players congratulate him on the accomplishment.

"I got a little emotional, because you may not know all those guys [in the video], but you've got a connection, because you played here and you're part of something that I consider a family," he said.

Hansbrough, who also grabbed nine rebounds, had already secured his place in Tar Heels history — and in the retired jersey portion of the Smith Center rafters, near Ford — by earning consensus national player-of-the-year honors last season.

Breaking such a long-standing record adds to his still-blooming legend.

Ford passed the likes of Lennie Rosenbluth, Charles Scott and Larry Miller because they could

LEFT: Tar Heel great Phil Ford congratulates Tyler Hansbrough (50) after he broke Ford's record for the most points scored in his career, after Hansbrough scored 20 points.
ROBERT WILLETT/THE NEWS & OBSERVER

BELOW: Tyler Hansbrough battles for a loose ball with Evansville's Kavon Lacey (2). ROBERT WILLETT/THE NEWS & OBSERVER

play varsity basketball for only three years. Antawn Jamison, Michael Jordan and Rashad McCants failed to pass Ford because they stayed just three seasons.

Then came Hansbrough, the sometimes awkward-looking big man from Poplar Bluff, Mo., who opted to forgo going to the NBA after his freshman, sophomore and junior seasons to try to win an NCAA title. Although he said he was a little nervous straying from the lane his rookie season, he actually scored his first Tar Heels bucket on Nov. 19, 2005, when he led a three-on-two fast break against Gardner-Webb that finished with his jump shot in the lane.

And he has barely slowed since, topping UNC's chart for all-time free-throw attempts — he passed the 1,000 mark Thursday night — en route to his latest record.

"I wanted it on a 3," Hansbrough said of the record-setting bucket, "but in a game, I realize you have to do what you have to do."

Which in his case, means playing with power and honing his improving finesse. If he remains healthy, the combination probably will help him become the ACC's all-time leading scorer, as well. Former Duke star J.J. Redick holds that mark with 2,769 points.

"I don't put anything past Tyler. If somebody tells me he's going to break the NBA scoring record — boy, that's going to be hard — but you never say never when it comes to Tyler," Gene Hansbrough said. "He's got a strong will."

And moves. ■

— Robbi Pickeral

OPPOSITE: UNC's Ty Lawson (5) leads a fast break in the first half against Rutgers. Lawson scored 19 points and had six assists.

ROBERT WILLETT/THE NEWS & OBSERVER

22

FRIDAY, DECEMBER 19, 2008

THE NEWS & OBSERVER

F ■ ■ ■ C

CLASSIFIED: Looking for something? Find the Classified section inside.

Sports

www.newsobserver.com/sports

COLTS RALLY
An emotional Jacksonville team can't hold off Indianapolis in the fourth quarter. **PAGE 14C**

‹ ANALYZING A DEAL
Staff writer Rick Bonnell takes a look at the Charlotte Bobcats' recent trade. **PAGE 8C**

| HURRICANES | | 2 |
| PANTHERS | (OT) | 1 |

Canes' Corvo nets OT winner

Back-to-back wins are first since November

By JAVIER SERNA
STAFF WRITER

RALEIGH – The Carolina Hurricanes could have let one get away.

But Joe Corvo scored his second straight winning goal and the Hurricanes escaped with a 2-1 overtime victory over the Florida Panthers before a reported crowd of 14,533 at the RBC Center on Thursday night.

The win produced Carolina's first back-to-back victory stretch since Nov. 21, and the Canes have earned at least one point in the past six games.

Rod Brind'Amour also collected assist No. 700 for his part in Corvo's goal, though it was Ray Whitney who fed Corvo.

"It's something when you're done and you look back it's nice to have these kinds of milestones," Brind'Amour said. "But the big thing was the win. We deserved that game, I thought. We gave up kind of an unlucky goal, really."

Corvo, pursued by defenders, took the puck to the right circle then moved back in front of the net, faking around David Booth and staying with the puck to backhand the winner between defender Keith Ballard, goalie Tomas Vokoun and center Gregory Campbell with 43.3 seconds left in overtime.

"Just a little patience," Corvo said. "I

SEE **HURRICANES**, PAGE 6C

The Hurricanes' Joe Corvo celebrates his winning goal with Ray Whitney and Frantisek Kaberle.
STAFF PHOTO BY CHRIS SEWARD

No 'what if': Wake kicker looks ahead

By EDWARD G. ROBINSON III
STAFF WRITER

WASHINGTON - Sam Swank fought the desire to do too much as he kicked 55-yard field goals during Wake Forest's Thursday morning practice.

He guarded against placing too much emotion into each kick, knowing none of them would bring back the time injury stole from him this football season.

NORTH CAROLINA 91, EVANSVILLE 73

2,302 and counting

WITH POWER MOVE, HANSBROUGH TAKES FORD'S UNC SCORING RECORD

As he has done so often, Tyler Hansbrough rises above the defense and launches a shot, this one making him the Tar Heels' all-time scoring leader.
STAFF PHOTOS BY ROBERT WILLETT

The Tar Heels and the Purple Aces play a game, but the attention is on record-setting UNC senior Tyler Hansbrough.

By ROBBI PICKERAL
STAFF WRITER

CHAPEL HILL – Since the day he stepped foot on North Carolina's campus, forward Tyler Hansbrough has been working to diversify his offensive résumé by trying to extend his shooting range.

But it seemed appropriate that when it came time to break UNC's three-decades-old career scoring record during the top-ranked Tar Heels' 91-73 basketball victory over Evansville on Thursday night, the senior went back to an old staple: a workmanlike power move.

With 7:42 left in the first half at the Smith Center, Hansbrough muscled around Purple Aces forwards James Haarsma and Pieter van Tongeren to bank in a shot off the glass and score his 10th point of the game and 2,292nd point of his career. That basket broke the mark of 2,290 that point guard Phil Ford set from 1974 to 1978.

Hansbrough finished with 20 points and now has 2,302 for his career.

"It was very fitting — three guys on him, he was moving to the basket, kind of off-balance, he banks it in with his soft hands," said Gene Hansbrough, who surprised his son by attending the game. "It was a perfect shot for Tyler to break the record on."

Point guard Ty Lawson also chipped in

16 points for the Tar Heels (10-0), though coach Roy Williams looked frustrated at times by his team's performance, particularly after Evansville's Shy Ely ended the first half with a dunk. That led the coach to stomp off the court despite the fact that his team led by 18 points.

The night, however, belonged to Hans-

brough, who accepted the game ball and an embrace from Ford, now an assistant coach for the NBA's Charlotte Bobcats, immediately after setting the record.

After the game, Ford pressed his hands together and bowed to the big man at mid-

SEE **UNC**, PAGE 4C

Phil Ford, who held UNC's scoring record for three decades, congratulates new record-holder Tyler Hansbrough during a break to present the ball.

UNC'S CAREER SCORING LEADERS

1. Tyler Hansbrough '05-present		2,302
2. Phil Ford	1974-78	2,290
3. Sam Perkins	1980-84	2,145
4. Lennie Rosenbluth	1954-57	2,045
5. Al Wood	1977-81	2,015
6. Charles Scott	1967-70	2,007
7. Larry Miller	1965-68	1,982
8. Antawn Jamison	1995-98	1,974
9. Brad Daugherty	1982-86	1,912
10. Walter Davis	1973-77	1,863

SOURCE: UNC

PHOTO GALLERIES

See more images and a First Look from the game.

■ Also, see a video of Tyler Hansbrough breaking the UNC scoring record and images from his career.

newsobserver.com/multimedia

INSIDE

GAME-BY-GAME LIST: How Tyler Hansbrough piled up his points. ▶ 4C

Typical bucket highlights atypical college career

Heels roll to 12-0

North Carolina vs. Rutgers // W 97-75   December 28, 2008

CHAPEL HILL — It started as a rumble, then escalated into a thunderous roar when Marcus Ginyard peeled off his warmup shirt and stepped onto the court Sunday night.

"Marcus Ginyard! Marcus Ginyard!" shouted the Smith Center crowd, now on its feet welcoming back North Carolina's senior.

Having missed the first 11 games after suffering a bone fracture in his left foot, Ginyard logged 11 minutes as the No. 1-ranked Tar Heels rebuffed pesky Rutgers 97-75.

Was he the same Ginyard who won the team's Defensive Player of the Year award the last two years? No.

Was he vocally positioning teammates like he's also known for doing? Not as much.

But he was out there for brief spells in both halves for the Tar Heels, who recorded their 12th straight double-digit victory, a school-record streak.

Ginyard didn't have to carry a big load. Tyler Hansbrough (26 points, 10 rebounds), Ty Lawson (19 points, 6 assists, 0 turnovers) and Danny Green (18 points) did their usual heavy lifting.

But Ginyard needed to get back in the fray, get the feel of things, get his footing, so to speak. He can augment a Carolina defense that is sagging a little. He can provide leadership. He can do "all those little things," coach Roy Williams said.

"He's about 80 percent, but I wanted to get him a few minutes," Williams said. "It's going to take time to get him in game shape. [But] it was fun to have him out there."

On his first foray on the court, he rebounded an air ball for a basket, deflected a pass, and manned up on his opponent. In the second half, he got a quick steal and fed the flying Lawson for a fastbreak layup.

His numbers read: 3 points, 4 re-

bounds, 2 steals. He also airballed a free throw, a sign of being winded.

"You get a little tired," Ginyard said. "[But] it was exciting to be on the court. I've got to get back to moving the same way, got to work to get up to game speed."

Before going in the game, Ginyard went to the tunnel and rode a stationary bike, like Dennis Rodman used to do. But biking isn't really his bag. He hopes he can soon bypass that activity before taking the floor.

Sitting for Ginyard — who had surgery on Oct. 8 — was tough. He was touched by the crowd response, saying "it's great to have fans [like that]." Teammates applauded as well.

"Marcus gives us a great threat, especially on the defensive end, where we need it," said Green. "He also tells guys where they need to be. He's vocal, good at talking to guys, a leader. It was good to see him move. He was doing okay."

Still, most of the night Ginyard watched as Hansbrough, Lawson, Green and the host of Tar Heels fought back a Scarlet Knights (9-4) team that offered more resistance than many expected.

Led by Mike Rosario's 26 points, Rutgers shot 47.5 percent against a UNC defense that gambled with traps and left some open spaces.

Yet the Tar Heels, who methodically built a 52-38 lead, maintained a double-digit spread throughtout the second half as Williams employed 10 players.

Nobody was as overwhelming as Hansbrough, who muscled around the basket and also stepped out to swish mid-ranger jumpers.

Lawson sped up and down the court with the zip and flair of, say, West Virginia quarterback Pat White. And Green — who was shown doing a Jingle Bells duet on

the scoreboard prior to the game with Deon Thompson — went 8-for-11popping from long range and delivering a few dunks.

As expected the Tar Heels won the battle of the boards, gaining a 50-26 rebounding advantage. And they piled up points in transition, as usual. All that, along with Ginyard's first appearance of the season, generally kept the Tar Heel loyalists in a joyful holiday mood. ■

— A.J. Carr

ABOVE: UNC's Ty Lawson (5) comes out of the game after scoring 19 points and handing out six assists against Rutgers. ROBERT WILLETT/ THE NEWS & OBSERVER

RIGHT: UNC's Danny Green (14) takes flight to the basket for a second half dunk. ROBERT WILLETT/THE NEWS & OBSERVER

OPPOSITE: Boston College's Reggie Jackson (0) blocks a shot attempt by UNC's Wayne Ellington. ROBERT WILLETT/THE NEWS & OBSERVER

Dean Dome debacle;
No. 1 team in the country finds itself at the bottom of ACC standings

North Carolina vs. Boston College // L 85-78 — **January 4, 2009**

CHAPEL HILL — It's one thing to lose a basketball game because you didn't shoot particularly well — or to have a 13-game winning streak snapped because you couldn't score enough points off turnovers — or to have a shot at an undefeated season end because you missed out on grabbing a rebound or two.

But it's another thing to be beaten — as top-ranked North Carolina was by Boston College, 85-78 on Sunday — because, according to several Tar Heels players, "we just weren't physical enough."

"It hurts," junior wing guard Wayne Ellington said. "It hurts a lot, especially from an upperclassmen viewpoint where we've been here before and we know what it takes, and we know how tough we need to play when the league comes around."

The Eagles, picked to finish 11th in the league's preseason poll, boxed out, shot through and slowed down UNC's dominant reputation because they were simply more aggressive from the outset at the Smith Center.

BC grabbed 13 of its 16 offensive rebounds in the first half, frustrated point guard Ty Lawson into his most mediocre game of the season (10 points, four assists, four turnovers) and built a lead that was too much for the Tar Heels to overcome even when they did find their physicality, and comeback mojo, in the closing minutes.

"I don't think anybody's really out-physicalled us — and I don't know if that's even a word — until today in the first half," UNC coach Roy Williams said. "But I thought we were just standing, and

MONDAY, JANUARY 5, 2009 — THE NEWS & OBSERVER — A ■ ■ ■ C +

Sports
www.newsobserver.com/sports

PACK WOMEN FALL
Associate head coach Stephanie Glance, left, and NCSU carry on without coach Kay Yow, who missed her fourth straight game Sunday. State lost at the buzzer to South Carolina. **PAGE 5C**

DUKE 69
VA. TECH 44

Devils roll in opener

Defense steps up in second half

BY J.P. GIGLIO
STAFF WRITER

DURHAM — No matter how the ACC season ends, Duke can make one claim that UNC can't — the Blue Devils won their conference opener.

Duke started ACC play with a 69-44 home win over Virginia Tech on Sunday night, tipping off minutes after Boston College stunned the Tar Heels 85-78 in Chapel Hill.

A vintage Duke defensive effort, holding the Hokies to 13 points in the second half, and 19 points from Kyle Singler made sure the Blue Devils didn't follow the Heels into the loss column.

Matching 14-2 runs — one in each half — gave the Devils a relatively comfortable win in what has been a competitive series since the Hokies joined the ACC.

Duke now leads 5-2.

Virginia Tech won the last meeting between the two at Cameron Indoor Stadium in January 2007, beating then-No. 5 Duke 69-67 in overtime. The Hokies couldn't repeat the upset of the No. 5 team in the country.

Duke responded to Virginia Tech's biggest threat — scoring the first four points of the second half to make it 39-35 — by rattling off 14 of the next 16 points.

By the time Duke made it 64-42 at the 6:10 mark, Virginia Tech coach Seth Greenberg had no choice but to call a timeout, prompting Duke coach Mike Krzyzewski to greet his team on the floor with a round of applause.

The Devils' man defense held A.D. Vassallo, Tech's leading scorer averaging 19 points per game, to seven points and forced

SEE DUKE, PAGE 4C

Gerald Henderson's strong all-around game for Duke included 15 points.
STAFF PHOTO BY CHUCK LIDDY

BOSTON COLLEGE 85, NORTH CAROLINA 78

Dean Dome debacle

NO. 1 TEAM IN THE COUNTRY FINDS ITSELF AT THE BOTTOM OF ACC STANDINGS

BY ROBBI PICKERAL
STAFF WRITER

CHAPEL HILL — It's one thing to lose a basketball game because you didn't shoot particularly well — or to have a 13-game winning streak snapped because you couldn't score enough points off turnovers — or to have a shot at an undefeated season end because you missed out on grabbing a rebound or two.

But it's another thing to be beaten, as top-ranked North Carolina was by Boston College, 85-78 on Sunday, because, according to several Tar Heels players, "we just weren't physical enough."

"It hurts," junior wing guard Wayne Ellington said. "It hurts a lot, especially from an upperclassmen viewpoint where we've been here before and we know what it takes, and we know how tough we need to play when the league comes around."

The Eagles, picked to finish 11th in the league's preseason poll, boxed out, shot through and slowed down UNC's dominant reputation because they were simply more aggressive from the outset at the Smith Center.

BC grabbed 13 of its 16 offensive rebounds in the first half, frustrated point guard Ty Lawson into his most mediocre game of the season (10 points, four assists, four turnovers) and built a lead that was too much for the Tar Heels to overcome even when they did find their physicality, and comeback mojo, in the closing minutes.

"I don't think anybody's really out-physicalled us — and I don't know if that's even a word — until today in the first half," UNC coach Roy Williams said. "But I thought we were just standing, and they were going after it."

Such as the time (or three) that BC grabbed three offensive rebounds before scoring. Or when the Eagles forced a jump ball with UNC forward Deon Thompson on the sideline because, as Williams put it, "you won't be aggressive and rip the ball through and to get the guy off of you."

North Carolina (13-1, 0-1 ACC) trailed at halftime for the first time this season, 46-40, after the Eagles outscored it 21-8 over the final 6:07 of the opening half.

UNC used All-American Tyler Hansbrough (21 points, nine

SEE UNC, PAGE 4C

PHOTO GALLERIES

See more images and a First Look from the game.
newsobserver.com/multimedia

Tyrese Rice, who scored 25 points, savors Boston College's imminent victory with four seconds left on the clock.
STAFF PHOTO BY ROBERT WILLETT

Tar Heels prove to be an imperfect team

Luke DeCock

CHAPEL HILL — By the end, North Carolina was reduced to heaving up 3-pointers in a parody of the way their previous opponents this season often ended up playing against the Tar Heels after all their other options are taken away.

In a season where the Heels have imposed their will with impunity, they found out what it's like to be imposed upon.

Carolina may have cruised through the first half of the schedule, but its first half for an undefeated season didn't survive the ACC opener. Boston College thoroughly and comprehensively beating the Tar Heels in an 85-78 win that wasn't as close as the final score.

From the unanimous No. 1 national ranking to a tie for last place in the ACC, all in the space of a Sunday afternoon where nothing went as planned for North Carolina.

"Nobody's incapable of losing," Carolina forward Danny Green said. "We're human, too. We're allowed to lose and things of that nature."

With Ty Lawson scoring his 1,000th point and Raymond Felton, Sean May and Marvin Williams all looking on from behind the Carolina bench, this had the feel of a coronation as the Heels took their first ACC step toward an undefeated season.

May's father Scott and his Indiana teammates are the last team to finish a college basketball season undefeated, in 1976. UNC won't have that opportunity now. The Heels were outgunned from the outside and outmuscled on the inside, although they were undone primarily by a 16-4 Boston College run midway through the second half that turned a two-point BC lead into a 14-point lead.

Nine of Boston College's points during that run were scored by a 6-3 freshman guard with the appropriate name of Reggie Jackson. Mr. January 4th finished with 17 points off the bench,

SEE DECOCK, PAGE 4C

RAVENS 27, DOLPHINS 9

Ravens defense ends Miami's resurgence

BY STEVEN WINE
THE ASSOCIATED PRESS

MIAMI — The Baltimore Ravens had Chad Pennington spinning, ducking, on his heels and on his back. When he did manage to get a pass away, they were often there to match it.

The Ravens came up with four interceptions, including one returned 64 yards for a touchdown by Ed Reed, and won 27-9 on Sunday to spoil the Miami Dolphins' first playoff game in seven seasons.

Baltimore stuffed Miami's ground attack and negated the Wildcat, but most of all the Ravens harried Pennington into uncharacteristic mistakes. After throwing only seven interceptions during the regular season, he had four during a 22-minute flurry midway through the game.

"We heard all week that they don't turn the ball over," linebacker Ray Lewis said. "But we force turnovers."

With a rookie coach in John Harbaugh and a rookie quarterback in Joe Flacco, wild-card entrant Baltimore (12-5) won for the 10th time in 12 games and will play Saturday at AFC South

SEE RAVENS, PAGE 6C

AFC Playoffs

SATURDAY, JAN. 10
Baltimore at Tennessee, 4:30 p.m.
(WRAL, WNCT)

SUNDAY, JAN. 11
San Diego at Pittsburgh, 4:45 p.m.
(WRAL, WNCT)

EAGLES 26, VIKINGS 14

Westbrook dash propels Eagles to win

BY DAVE CAMPBELL
THE ASSOCIATED PRESS

MINNEAPOLIS — All but forgotten as postseason contenders, Donovan McNabb and the Philadelphia Eagles have a playoff win.

Brian Westbrook caught a short pass out of the backfield and zigzagged through the Minnesota defense for a devastating 71-yard touchdown midway through the fourth quarter, and the Eagles spoiled the Vikings' first home playoff game in eight years with a 26-14 victory Sunday.

"I've seen this team have confidence in each other and try to have one another's back," McNabb said. "What you're seeing is a team playing with a lot of energy, playing with emotion, and just having fun."

Asante Samuel's 44-yard interception return of Tarvaris Jackson's errant pass in the second quarter set a tone for the kind of game most Vikings fans feared from the unpolished quarterback.

Andy Reid improved his playoff coaching record to 9-6, including at least one win each time the Eagles have qualified in his 10 years. He bested his buddy and former offensive coordinator Brad Childress in this one, and they spoke for several moments on the field after the game while maybe a thousand Eagles fans cheered

SEE EAGLES, PAGE 6C

Philadelphia's DeSean Jackson (10) turns upfield during a 62-yard punt return in the first quarter on Sunday.
AP PHOTO BY ANN HEISENFELT

NFC Playoffs

SATURDAY, JAN. 10
Arizona at Carolina, 8:15 p.m. (WRAZ, WFXI)

SUNDAY, JAN. 11
Philadelphia at N.Y. Giants, 1 p.m. (WRAZ, WFXI)

25

they were going after it."

Such as the time (or three) that BC grabbed three offensive rebounds before scoring. Or when the Eagles forced a jump ball with UNC forward Deon Thompson on the sideline because, as Williams put it, "you won't be aggressive and rip the ball through and to get the guy off of you."

Added Williams: "We didn't do a very good job of attacking. We've got to be more physical, we've got to be tougher mentally and physically and all those things."

North Carolina (13-1, 0-1 ACC) trailed at halftime for the first time this season, 46-40, after the Eagles

(13-2, 1-0) outscored the Tar Heels 21-9 over the final 6:07 of the opening half.

Tyler Hansbrough (21 points, nine rebounds) helped UNC cut the deficit to 58-56 in the opening minutes of the second half, only to have BC unleash a 16-4 run during which Reggie Jackson scored nine points to make it 74-60 with 9:24 remaining.

"There's no question that we kind of kept it at our pace, at least as far as I'm concerned. On the offensive end [we] did what we wanted to do," BC coach Al Skinner said.

Trailing 78-63 with 6:07 remaining, UNC tried to regain its ag-

gressiveness, forcing turnovers and grabbing rebounds to feed a 15-4 run that cut the deficit to 82-78 with 47 seconds left. But Eagles point guard Tyrese Rice (25 points, eight assists), who anchored his team all night, hit two free throws with 27.7 seconds left. UNC's Ellington and Danny Green each missed 3-point tries before Rice buried another free throw to seal it.

UNC shot 29.3 percent in the second half and 38.4 percent for the game. Its five points off turnovers were a season low.

"I do believe that Tyler is one of the more physical players, and I think our guys can be, and they

were [during] the last five or six minutes," Williams said. "But you can't spot a good team with a ball-control guard [Rice] that kind of lead and expect them to roll over and play dead for you."

Ellington said his team knew — or should have known — that the competition would ramp up against ACC foes. But he also said the team "got comfortable" after beating its first 13 opponents by an average of 26.4 points.

"It's a wake-up call," he said. "We take that hit on the chin, and you learn from it and grow from it and bounce back." ∎

— Robbi Pickeral

Heels finally get it going;
Second-half surge swamps Cougars

North Carolina vs. C of Charleston // W 108-70   January 7, 2009

CHAPEL HILL — Well, that's more like it.

Three days after losing its No. 1 ranking, its first game of the season and its chance to go undefeated, No. 3 North Carolina bounced back Wednesday with a 108-70 blowout of College of Charleston at the Smith Center.

The Tar Heels' defense wasn't suffocating, what with the Cougars shooting 46.9 percent in the first half and one of UNC's best stoppers, Marcus Ginyard, sitting on the bench for the entire game. But Carolina shot much better from the field (58.6 percent) and the free-throw line (19-for-22) — and became the first opponent to score 100 or more points against the Cougars since 1977, a span of 951 games.

Plus, there was no questioning the Tar Heels' aggressiveness. Their lack of that was something they believe cost them dearly in their loss to Boston College on Sunday.

"We wanted to get some of that out of our system — some of that feeling of disappointment, by coming out and playing well tonight," UNC forward Tyler Hansbrough said. "It's still going to be there, but it helps that we came out and won and played well."

Considering Charleston led by as many as three points early, then remained within striking distance for most of the first half by burying eight 3-pointers, it wasn't exactly the rout in the beginning UNC fans might have expected.

But Carolina (14-1), which made 59.5 percent of its shots in the first period, pulled away with an 8-2 run — including a Ty Lawson layup at the horn — to take a 53-41 lead into halftime.

The Tar Heels began the second period with an 11-0 run and the Cougars (10-3) never really recovered.

Reserve point guard Larry Drew II's layup with 3:51 left gave the Tar Heels a 100-60 lead, and marked the first time since Dec. 6, 1977, that the Cougars allowed an opponent to score in triple digits; it was the second-longest such streak in the nation.

"I could care less about that," Cougars coach Bobby Cremins said of the streak.

"... There's no excuses. I thought we could've played better. They're good. Also, after Boston College, I knew they would be totally focused."

And they managed that focus without Ginyard, who returned last month after having foot surgery in October. He played in the previous three games but has been slow to return to 100 percent. He was in uniform, but UNC coach Roy Williams said: "I didn't feel like playing him tonight; he's been struggling quite a bit, and he's just not where

RIGHT: UNC's Ed Davis (32) shoots over College of Charleston's Jermaine Johnson (5). ROBERT WILLETT/ THE NEWS & OBSERVER

OPPOSITE: Boston College's Joe Trapani (12) goes after a loose ball with UNC's Ty Lawson (5) late in the second half. ROBERT WILLETT/THE NEWS & OBSERVER

we wanted him to be at that time and decided not to play him."

The senior went through pre-game warm-ups, then sat on the bench wearing a sleeve on his right leg to protect a lingering knee bruise.

Asked if Ginyard's problems had to do with his previously broken left foot, or getting back into game shape, Williams said: "It's everything. Have you seen the offensive rebounds, have you seen the steals, have you seen the kinds of plays Marcus makes his living on? I haven't either. So we're trying to give him a little more time and see what happens."

Hansbrough led the team with 24 points and seven rebounds. Deon Thompson and Lawson chipped in 15 points apiece. Shooting guard Wayne Ellington, who had made only 29 of 79 shots in his previous seven home games, finished 3-for-5 with 10 points.

Tony White Jr. led Charleston with 16 points.

"Basically, for us, it was an opportunity to get the bad taste out of our mouth," Williams said. ∎

— Robbi Pickeral

LEFT: UNC's Deon Thompson (21) shoots over College of Charleston's Jermaine Johnson (5) in the first half. ROBERT WILLETT/THE NEWS & OBSERVER

FAR LEFT: UNC's Wayne Ellington (22) defends College of Charleston's Marcus Hammond (31) in the first half. ROBERT WILLETT/THE NEWS & OBSERVER

Deacons handle Heels;
UNC falls to 0-2 in ACC

North Carolina vs. ⁴Wake Forest // L 92-89   January 11, 2009

WINSTON-SALEM — Was it only eight days ago that fans were talking about the possibility of North Carolina going undefeated? About how its starting point guard was playing the best basketball of his career?

About where this the team might end up ranking among the school's all-time best?

Now, Wake Forest faithful might start pondering the same things about their squad.

Led by 34 points from their star ball-handler, Jeff Teague, the fourth-ranked Demon Deacons outshot, outpaced and downright outplayed No. 3 UNC, winning 92-89 on Sunday at Joel Coliseum.

The Demon Deacons (14-0, 1-0 ACC) remained one of three undefeated teams in the country. Carolina (14-2, 0-2), which had its 15-game road winning streak snapped, hasn't lost its first two league games since 1996-97; that team began conference play 0-3 before advancing to the Final Four.

But this current Tar Heels team looks far from that right now.

"Sometimes we go out there and just expect to win instead of realizing that nobody's going to roll over for us; we've got a target on our back," shooting guard Wayne Ellington said. "I feel like we've got to get a little more hungry — we've got to want it more, we've got to go take it instead of thinking that somebody's going to just give it to us."

The only thing Wake "gave" the Tar Heels on Sunday was 11 missed free throws and a 14-rebound deficit.

And a lot of headaches.

With the team's best wing defender, Marcus Ginyard, sitting on the bench trying to rest a lingering foot injury, Teague took advantage of everyone who tried to guard him — including Ty Lawson, Ellington, Bobby Frasor and Larry Drew II. It marked the ACC lead-

ing scorer's second straight game with 30 points or more.

"I told Jeff Teague — and I mean it — that that was as good a performance in a long time against a team I'm coaching," UNC coach Roy Williams said. "I thought he was sensational."

Meanwhile, Lawson (9 points, 5 assists, 4 turnovers) got outplayed for his second consecutive league game. UNC forward

---

MONDAY, JANUARY 12, 2009   THE NEWS & OBSERVER   r ■ ■ ■ C +

Sports
www.newsobserver.com/sports

STILL WINNING
Dwight Howard leads the NBA's Orlando Magic to its 13th win in 15 games. PAGE 8C

‹ ONE MORE TIME
Quarterback Tim Tebow says he will play his senior season at Florida. PAGE 5C

UNC WOMEN	75
NCSU (OT)	66

Hatchell wins No. 800

By Edward G. Robinson III
STAFF WRITER

CHAPEL HILL — As her players launched off-the-mark 3-pointers and N.C. State kept the game close, North Carolina women's basketball coach Sylvia Hatchell said she thought history would have to wait on Sunday.

INSIDE
SUBS: Deep bench helps Duke women succeed. **• 5C**

"I was about to think it wasn't going to happen," she said to a cheering crowd of 7,010 at the Smith Center moments after her team edged the Wolfpack 75-66 in overtime and made her 800th career victory official.

Hatchell became just the fourth coach in NCAA Division I women's basketball to collect 800 victories. She joined Tennessee's Pat Summitt, Rutgers' Vivian Stringer and former Texas coach Jody Conradt. Hatchell's record, after 34 seasons overall and 22 at UNC, is 800-274.

UNC's victory set off a trip down memory lane for Hatchell, who stood at center court with athletic director Dick Baddour and watched a video montage of her feats, with former colleagues and

SEE **800**, PAGE 4C

Rivals unite in tribute

CHAPEL HILL — At noon, an hour before they would resume their women's basketball rivalry, the players and coaches for N.C. State and North Carolina stood together at center court, arms interlocked in an unbroken circle of love.

Throughout the ACC and across the country, wherever Kay Yow's name is spoken with admiration, others were doing the same — a midday prayer for the health of the Wolfpack women's basketball coach, who was absent Sunday but who cast, as always, a tall shadow.

Yow's seat at the end of the N.C. State bench sat unoccupied throughout the 75-66 overtime loss to Carolina on Sunday. There's nothing new about that, as Yow has missed dozens of games during

SEE **DECOCK**, PAGE 4C

WAKE FOREST 92, NORTH CAROLINA 89

Deacons handle Heels

TEAGUE SCORES CAREER-HIGH 34 POINTS; UNC FALLS TO 0-2 IN ACC

By Robbi Pickeral
STAFF WRITER

WINSTON-SALEM — Was it only eight days ago that fans were talking about the possibility of North Carolina going undefeated? About how its starting point guard was playing the best basketball of his career?

About where this the team might end up ranking among the school's all-time best?

Now, Wake Forest faithful might start pondering the same things about their squad.

Led by 34 points from their star ball-handler, Jeff Teague, the fourth-ranked Demon Deacons outshot, outpaced and downright outplayed No. 3 UNC, winning 92-89 on Sunday at Joel Coliseum.

The Demon Deacons (14-0, 1-0 ACC) remained one of three undefeated teams in the country. Carolina (14-2, 0-2), which had its 15-game road winning streak snapped, hasn't lost its first two league games since 1996-97; that team began conference play 0-3 before advancing to the Final Four.

But this current Tar Heels team looks far from that right now.

"Sometimes we go out there and just expect to win instead of

SEE **UNC**, PAGE 4C

Wake Forest's Jeff Teague drives to the basket against North Carolina's Ed Davis at Joel Coliseum in Winston-Salem.
STAFF PHOTO BY ROBERT WILLETT

Soft Heels must toughen up

WINSTON-SALEM — One way or another, North Carolina's basketball season was defined Sunday night, and that's not to say Wake Forest isn't the best team in the college gym.

It's entirely possible, at this point, that the Deacons are just flat-out, plain better than the Tar Heels. Certainly, that conclusion is there to be drawn from Wake's emphatic 92-89 win in Joel Coliseum.

What is certain is the Tar Heels, listed as nine-point favorites entering the game but now 0-2 in the ACC, are a far cry from the monolithic power that almost everyone envisioned before the season.

SEE **TUDOR**, PAGE 4C

EAGLES 23, GIANTS 11

Defensive Eagles dethrone Giants

By Ben Walker
THE ASSOCIATED PRESS

EAST RUTHERFORD, N.J. – Donovan McNabb will get another chance to chase that elusive Super Bowl title. Eli Manning threw away his opportunity to defend it.

McNabb made all the big plays that Manning did not, and the Philadelphia Eagles eliminated the New York Giants 23-11 on Sunday to reach the NFC title game for the fifth time in eight seasons.

"He is the best quarterback in the NFL," Eagles coach Andy Reid praised his guy. "I don't think I have to say anything more than that."

Manning, meanwhile, never resembled the poised quarterback who won last year's Super Bowl MVP award with that one perfect

spiral to Plaxico Burress.

Five times New York got inside the Eagles' 20. The result? A mere three field goals.

"When we needed to get something done, get a spark to make a big play, that's when we didn't do our best," Manning said.

Credit Philadelphia's hard-hitting, ball-hawking defense, and maybe blame the wind gusts a bit. Either way, these NFL playoffs are now for the Birds — the underdog Eagles, Cardinals and Ravens all won on the road this weekend.

McNabb lunged for one touchdown, threw for another and converted several key third downs to move the sixth-seeded Eagles

SEE **EAGLES**, PAGE 7C

STEELERS 35, CHARGERS 24

Steelers shut down Sproles & Co.

Pittsburgh keeps home field an advantage and sets up showdown with Ravens

Pittsburgh's Willie Parker looks for room to run against San Diego's Cletis Gordon. Parker rushed for 146 yards.
GETTY IMAGES PHOTO BY CHRIS GRAYTHEN

By Alan Robinson
THE ASSOCIATED PRESS

PITTSBURGH – Fittingly enough, the Pittsburgh Steelers brought back the home-field advantage to the NFL playoffs. Now they get to stay at home for the AFC championship game and take on the rival they dislike more than any other.

INSIDE
PANTHERS: The offseason drama begins for Carolina. **• 6C**

The team with the NFL's best home-field record since the 1970 NFL merger shook off a 7-0 deficit barely two minutes into the game, shut down pint-sized playmaker Darren Sproles and returned some normality to the NFL playoffs by beating the San Diego

Chargers 35-24 in an AFC divisional game Sunday.

With now-healthy Willie Parker running for 146 yards and two touchdowns, and Ben Roethlisberger ignoring his late-season concussion to throw for a touchdown and lead an efficient offense, the Steelers did what the favored Tennessee Titans, Carolina Panthers and New York Giants couldn't do by winning at home. It was the first time since 1971 that three road teams won during a playoff weekend, and the Steelers made certain that road teams didn't go 4-for-4.

The Steelers had the worst offense of any playoff team coming in, only to put up 35 points to

SEE **STEELERS**, PAGE 7C

Deon Thompson (eight points) struggled again. And All-American Tyler Hansbrough (17 points, 11 rebounds), who was harassed by an array of Deacons 6 feet 9 or taller, actually got outscored by Chas McFarland (20 points).

"They swarmed me, they played physical ... but that's the way the game's played sometimes," Hansbrough said. "... I just try to play my game."

The Tar Heels didn't actually manage to play their game — meaning hitting shots and getting to the free throw line — until the final minutes, though.

The score was tied 44-44 at half-time, and UNC got its final lead at the 18:37 mark, when Ellington buried two free throws.

Three Ellington free throws with 1:16 left put the Heels back into contention, cutting Wake's lead to 87-83. But Teague hit three free throws down the stretch to seal the victory.

In all, four Tar Heel starters — Ellington, Ty Lawson, Tyler Hansbrough and Deon Thompson — made only 14 of their combined 50 shots. Danny Green, who led the team with 22 points, was 6-for-9.

"Obviously, we're mad right now about some things," Hansbrough said. "... But we just need to get back to practice and start playing again." ■

— Robbi Pickeral

LEFT: UNC coach Roy Williams shows frustration at his team's poor play. ROBERT WILLETT/THE NEWS & OBSERVER

OPPOSITE: UNC's Deon Thompson (21) reacts to a Tar Heel turnover, as Wake Forest's Chas McFarland (13) applauds. ROBERT WILLETT/THE NEWS & OBSERVER

The Home Stretch: Second Half of the Season

January 21, 2009 - March 14, 2009

Heels streak to easy win; Ellington helps send Clemson to its 54th straight loss in Chapel Hill

North Carolina vs. ¹⁰Clemson // W 94-70   January 21, 2009

CHAPEL HILL — Wayne Ellington continues to have Clemson's number.

This time, it was 25.

Once again, the North Carolina sharpshooter was more disruptive to the Tigers' game plan than All-American Tyler Hansbrough, leading the fifth-ranked Tar Heels to a 94-70 victory Wednesday to keep Clemson 0-for-forever (technically, 0-for-54) against UNC in Chapel Hill.

It remains the longest streak of home basketball wins over one opponent in NCAA history.

"I don't know what it is, but he always seems to do well against us," Clemson forward Trevor Booker said.

Ellington's season-high 25 points at the Smith Center marked the first time in his college career that he has posted back-to-back 20-point games, and it continued his Tiger-taming trend.

Last season at Clemson, he capped his career-high 36-point performance with a winning 3-pointer. Later that season, at the Smith Center, he swished 28 points, including five 3-pointers. During the ACC Tournament matchup, he scored 24.

"Maybe he doesn't like the color orange," UNC coach Roy Williams said of Ellington's continued success over the Tigers. "I think some styles of game fit certain players, and it's up and down and we have a point guard and others who can find Wayne."

After breaking out of a frustrating cold spell by draining seven straight 3-pointers against Miami on Saturday, Ellington tormented the No. 10 Tigers in a number of ways.

He opened the game with a 3-pointer to knot the score 3-3. Then, with his team trailing 38-36, he scored five points during a 9-2 run to close the first half. One field goal came on a fastbreak dunk, the other on a 3-pointer, to give UNC (17-2, 3-2 ACC) a 45-40 advantage at halftime.

And the only reason Clemson (16-2, 2-2) — which led by as many as five points in the first half but had its fullcourt defense shredded on a regular basis — was even close at the half was guard Terrence Oglesby. He opened the game with a 3-pointer and was 3-for-6 from behind the arc with 17 points at the break.

"With Tywon [Lawson] being as fast as he is and being able to break down the press, and I just get open looks all night long," said Ellington, who made nine of his 15 shots for the game. "And that just gets me going. Once I get one or two open looks, I think I'm gone from there."

Ellington continued torching the Tigers after halftime, scoring four points — on a putback, in transition, and on a drive — during a 10-2 second-half opening run from which Clemson never recovered.

The rest of the Tar Heels added highlights after that, holding the Tigers to 10-for-35 shooting in the second half while Hansbrough

recorded another double-double (20 points, 10 rebounds), and Deon Thompson secured his first double-figure scoring outing against an ACC foe this season (he finished with 15).

"We talked to our team about transition defense, and we talked about Ellington getting those easy run-outs — they're much more dangerous than him shooting 3s," said Clemson coach Oliver Purnell, whose team allowed the most points it has given up all season. "And again, we didn't do either, whether it was getting back to contest their bigs — inside, they run so well — or those run-outs by Ellington."

Lawson added 16 for UNC, and Ellington had a career-high seven assists.

"There are so many good players on that team, what can you do?" Oglesby asked. "When you play Carolina, you really can't focus on one." ∎

— Robbi Pickeral

LEFT: UNC's Tyler Hansbrough (50) gets a dunk over Clemson's Trevor Booker (35) with 5:20 left in regulation to pull the Tar Heels to within nine points, 66-75. ROBERT WILLETT/ THE NEWS & OBSERVER

PREVIOUS: UNC fans yell at Duke players as they head out onto the court at the Dean Smith Center in Chapel Hill for the March 8 game. CHUCK LIDDY/THE NEWS & OBSERVER

FOLLOWING LEFT: Deon Thompson (21) gets a power dunk over Clemson's Trevor Booker. ROBERT WILLETT/ THE NEWS & OBSERVER

FOLLOWING RIGHT: UNC's Ed Davis (32) shoots while defended by N.C. State's Tracy Smith (23) in the first half. ETHAN HYMAN/THE NEWS & OBSERVER

Psycho T back to form; North Carolina star rebounds with a 31-point effort

North Carolina vs. NC State // W 93-76   January 31, 2009

RALEIGH — Just before the national anthem, a particularly boisterous N.C. State fan broke the silence at the RBC Center by screaming "I hate you Tyler!"

Now the Wolfpack abhors him even more.

North Carolina forward Tyler Hansbrough fed off the constant taunts to lead his fifth-ranked team to its fifth straight victory in the series, this time 93-76.

His 31 points were the biggest X-factor in a duel that had all the hallmarks of the always-heated rivalry: an early double-digit lead, a late comeback attempt, and a couple of last-minute technicals that saw one player — UNC reserve Mike Copeland — escorted to the locker room early after responding to a hard foul by State's Ben McCauley.

"They outplayed us," said Wolf-pack coach Sidney Lowe, whose team was outrebounded by nine and shot 41.8 percent. "Their bigs outplayed us. That's it. They were tough inside, scored the ball inside."

The dominance began with Hansbrough, who had scored 17, 24 and 32 points in his three previous games here against State. Coming off his worst offensive performance of the season — eight points at Florida State on Wednesday — the senior said he was already fired up from the outset. Then he got an extra kick in the shorts when he was briefly benched.

"He didn't box out," UNC coach Roy Williams said, referring to a play when State's Brandon Costner grabbed a too-easy rebound. "I love him to death, and my gosh I've been the luckiest coach in America,

but anybody can box out or at least make an effort. He didn't so he got a chance to come over there and see what it feels like to be over there early."

Hansbrough obviously didn't like it, returning to the court and scoring 11 first-half points. But he was really just warming up.

"They decided to guard him one-on-one, which is crazy — [so we thought], 'Let's get him the ball,' " reserve guard Bobby Frasor said. "And he dominated the second half, hitting a 3 and jump shots, tip-shots, typical Tyler jump hooks in the post and at the free-throw line."

It was more than enough to with-stand a late comeback, led by State senior Courtney Fells. After scoring only two points in the first half, the guard swished in an additional 20 in the second, helping the Pack whittle a once-18-point deficit to 80-72 with 5:06 left.

"I believed we would win when we were down eight," Fell said. "But we got away from what we were do-ing and let them get the momentum back."

Indeed, Hansbrough followed a Deon Thompson jumper with one of his own to push his team's lead back to a dozen points, then his 3-pointer with 2:29 left gave the Tar Heels an insurmountable 89-72 advantage.

In the end, Hansbrough and UNC dominated up front with 46 points in the paint to N.C. State's 16. That was difficult for the Wolfpack (11-8, 2-5 ACC) to accept because post veterans Mc-Cauley (five points) and Brandon Costner (13 points) are supposed to be the team's strength. But Costner counted 11 missed layups by N.C. State, and McCauley took the blame for the defeat.

"I need to work on finishing around the basket," said McCauley,

who combined with big men Costner and Tracy Smith to shoot 8-for-27 from the field. "Those shots are going to fall and they have been falling, so we can go from here. We know maybe this is just a fluke."

Five players scored in double figures for Carolina (19-2, 5-2), which shot 56.5 percent. And Hansbrough's 12-for-17 performance wasn't a fluke. It marked his 70th 20-point conference game, tying Duke's J.J. Redick for the ACC record. It also marked his 118th game in double figures, tying the UNC record held by Sam Perkins.

Just another couple of reasons for N.C. State fans to hate him. If Saturday wasn't enough, that is.

"It adds a little more fuel to the fire," Hansbrough said of the taunts. "It's always good to beat a rival on their home court." ■

— Robbi Pickeral

LEFT TOP: Ty Lawson reacts after drawing a foul from N.C. State's Farnold Degand (12) and sinking the basket. ROBERT WILLETT/THE NEWS & OBSERVER

LEFT BOTTOM: Tyler Hansbrough gets an easy dunk, as teammate Deon Thompson (21), and N.C. State's Ben McCauley (34) looks on at the RBC Center. ROBERT WILLETT/THE NEWS & OBSERVER

OPPOSITE: N.C. State's Tracy Smith has his shot blocked by UNC's Tyler Hansbrough in the second half. ETHAN HYMAN/THE NEWS & OBSERVER

BELOW: UNC's Danny Green (14) blocks a shot by N.C. State's Tracy Smith (23) in the second half. ROBERT WILLETT/THE NEWS & OBSERVER

After UNC's frigid first half, Ellington and Lawson lead a decisive offensive surge

North Carolina vs. Virginia // W 76-61 February 7, 2009

CHAPEL HILL — In the end, it was the blowout most expected: North Carolina 76, Virginia 61.

It was just an awful ugly way to get there.

The third-ranked Tar Heels found about every way to miss shots early on at the Smith Center — clunks, airballs, toilet-bowl rolls right out of the rim — but they used solid defense and a second-half offensive surge to secure their seventh straight victory Saturday afternoon.

Their hope now is that they've shot out all the kinks (and clanks) in time for their showdown with No. 4 Duke on Wednesday night.

"I expect a classic rivalry game," said forward Tyler Hansbrough, who finished with 15 points and 13 rebounds. "Any time you go over to Duke, it's going to be a big-time game. Whether it's here or there, it's going to be hyped-up, and you have to bring your game."

The Tar Heels (21-2, 7-2 ACC), who made just 11 of their 33 shots in the first half, will want to take a much more accurate shooting performance to Cameron Indoor Stadium.

The last two times UNC made a third or fewer of their shots was in the second halves of their losses to Boston College (.293) and Wake Forest (.282).

This time around, Virginia used a 9-2 run to cut its deficit to 24-23 on a Jeff Jones field goal with 3:48 left in the first half. But UNC used concentrated defense (the Cavs shot 31.4 percent before halftime, and 36.5 percent for the game) and a 9-2 spurt of its own before intermission to regain control of the game.

"I thought they were [in] a lot of places, and sometimes it looked like there were more than five guys out there on the floor," Virginia coach Dave Leitao said. "We had opportunities, but what happens with good defensive teams, the opportunities that they give you; you're not real comfortable. So what happens is you end up missing a point-blank shot or something you're normally used to making. That's what they did do us today."

Leading 33-25 at the half, Carolina then opened the second half with a 7-0 run, and the Cavs never threatened after that.

"It was an unusual game because the first half was like pulling teeth; we couldn't get a shot to go in," coach Roy Williams said. "I thought we were doing OK on the defensive end, we just couldn't make anything. And then the first 16 minutes of the second half, I thought we were very good."

Wing guard Wayne Ellington led the Tar Heels with 20 points, six rebounds and six assists. Point guard Ty Lawson had 10 points, nine assists and zero turnovers.

And Williams was particularly pleased that Danny Green, who had been ill for the last couple of days, was able to play 28 minutes.

"At the 16-minute mark of warm-

ups I went out to Danny because I didn't even know if I was going to play him, and had to see what he felt like," Williams said. "He said he felt better, and they gave him some ibuprofen ... and then about a million gallons of some kind of liquid, I guess. I think it was important to get that out of him."

Jones led Virginia with 19 points. The Cavs (7-12, 1-7) have now lost seven straight.

Meanwhile, despite their poor shooting performance, the Tar Heels remain the hottest team in the league after opening ACC play 0-2. Just in time to face Duke.

"We just felt like we had to put it in [the hoop], get out in the passing lanes, get some easy ones — we've got to find a way," Ellington said. "... And we did." ∎

— Robbi Pickeral

LEFT: UNC's Wayne Ellington (22) drives to the basket past Virginia's Sylven Landesberg (15) in the second half. ROBERT WILLETT/THE NEWS & OBSERVER

OPPOSITE: UNC coach Roy Williams reacts to a foul against Deon Thompson (21) in the second half. ROBERT WILLETT/THE NEWS & OBSERVER

FOLLOWING LEFT: UNC head coach Roy Williams screams at his players in the second half of play at Cameron Indoor Stadium. CHUCK LIDDY/ THE NEWS & OBSERVER

FOLLOWING RIGHT: UNC's Ty Lawson (5) drives against Duke's Kyle Singler (12) for a lay-up in the second half. Lawson led all scorers with 25 points, and the Tar Heels to a 101-87 victory. ROBERT WILLETT/THE NEWS & OBSERVER

Lawson leads way;
UNC completes senior slam

North Carolina vs. ⁶Duke // W 101-87   February 11, 2009

DURHAM — North Carolina seniors Tyler Hansbrough and Danny Green will remember Wednesday as the night they completed their careers with a perfect record at Duke's Cameron Indoor Stadium.

The also ought to remember it as the night Ty Lawson stepped on the accelerator and willed the No. 3-ranked Tar Heels to a 101-87 defeat of No. 6 Duke.

Lawson was held to four points and two field goal attempts in the first half as the hot-shooting Blue

Devils ran out to a 52-44 lead. But after halftime, Duke couldn't find anybody to stop speedy junior point guard Lawson from getting into the lane.

"I barely went to the basket at all [in the first half]," Lawson said, "because it was really clogged up in the lane. Coach [Roy Williams] told me he wanted me to step up in the second half and get more aggressive."

Duke's switching on screens has kept opponents from penetrating for most of the season, but couldn't keep

Lawson from getting into the heart of the defense. He simply lowered his shoulder and used his strength to drive and bank the ball into the basket.

"Lawson was a pro tonight," said Duke coach Mike Krzyzewski. "That's as good as a point guard has played against us in a while."

Greg Paulus, who started at point guard for Duke, couldn't stop Lawson. Nolan Smith, the former starter who is a better defender than Paulus, couldn't stop Lawson and got in foul trouble trying to do it.

Lawson, who is known as one of the fastest players in college basketball, finished with 25 points.

"He scored 21 of his points in the second half," said forward Kyle Singler, whose 22 points led Duke. "That's going to kill you."

Lawson, who'd had 15 assists and no turnovers in the previous two games, helped move North Carolina (22-2, 8-2 ACC) into a spot many assumed the Tar Heels would occupy throughout the season — the top of the ACC standings.

After starting 0-2 in the confer-

ence, North Carolina broke a first-place tie with Duke (20-4, 7-3). The Tar Heels have won six of the last eight in the series, and Hansbrough and Green are the first North Carolina players to finish their careers 4-0 at Cameron during Mike Krzyzewski's 29 seasons as Duke's coach.

Just one week after being held to 47 points at Clemson, Duke suddenly became shockingly efficient on offense midway through the first half against the Tar Heels.

After Hansbrough fouled twice in 13 seconds in the 12th minute, the

Blue Devils scored 14 of 17 points as North Carolina's defense crumbled.

Jon Scheyer and Gerald Henderson both scored 13 first-half points as Duke reached halftime with a 52-44 lead, and more points than it scored in an entire game at Clemson.

But the Blue Devils shot just 2-for-15 from 3-point range in the second half after going 6-for-9 before halftime as North Carolina tightened up its defense.

When Lawson turned on the jets on offense, the Tar Heels scored 20 points more than any other team has scored against Duke this season. All five North Carolina starters scored at least 12.

And after the game was over, Lawson talked a little trash with the Duke students. He said he'd been holding it in for the whole game as they taunted him about his June arrest for driving after consuming alcohol.

"I had to let it out," Lawson said of the exchange with the students. ■

— Ken Tysiac

Lawson buries 3-pointers to bury Miami

North Carolina vs. Miami // W 69-65   February 15, 2009

CORAL GABLES, Fla. — Ty Lawson doesn't have anything to say to people who still doubt his outside shot.

He just continues to prove them wrong.

Sunday, for instance, the North Carolina point guard buried three key 3-pointers in the final 3:35 at BankUnited Center to help his team withstand a 35-point barrage by Miami's Jack McClinton and edge the Hurricanes 69-65.

Third-ranked UNC (23-2, 9-2 ACC) has now won nine straight since it started 0-2 in the league. It also now boasts a stranglehold on first place in the ACC standings, thanks to losses earlier in the day by Duke and Clemson.

Meanwhile, five of Miami's seven ACC losses have been decided by five points or less — including three in overtime.

"We know Ty can shoot lights-out, and he just stepped up for us; he was huge," said shooting guard Wayne Ellington, who recorded his first double-double (15 points, 10 rebounds) despite wearing a sleeve to protect pulled ligaments in his right arm. "We needed him to come in and be huge for us, and that's exactly what he did."

It was the third "huge" game-sealing performance by Lawson in three weeks, joining the buzzer-beating 3-pointer the speedy junior made to win at Florida State on Jan. 28 and his 21-point second-half at Duke on Wednesday.

And this time, the Tar Heels needed it to thwart the third guard this season to drop 30 or more points against them.

UNC had a comfortable-looking 54-40 with 12:01 left, thanks to a 19-7 run. But McClinton, the ACC's career leader in 3-point shooting percentage, made it interesting by scoring 12 points during a 17-4 run that cut UNC's lead to 58-57 with just under five minutes left.

After UNC's Danny Green blocked a shot by McClinton to keep Miami (15-9, 4-7) from pulling ahead, Lawson — who had been feeling sick since Thursday, but didn't look it — matched 3-pointers with Adrian Thompson and Mc-

---

RIGHT: UNC's Danny Green (14) battles with Duke's Gerald Henderson (15) for a rebound in the first half. ROBERT WILLETT/THE NEWS & OBSERVER

OPPOSITE: UNC fans celebrate on Franklin Street after Carolina defeats Duke. It was the first of two regular season matchups between the rival schools. JASON ARTHURS/THE NEWS & OBSERVER

Clinton to keep UNC clinging to a 64-63 lead.

Tar Heels forward Tyler Hansbrough, held to an unusually-low eight points, took a charge from Brian Asbury to keep the Hurricanes from pulling ahead.

Then Lawson buried his career-high fifth 3-pointer from about two steps beyond the arc to give his team a four-point cushion with 10 seconds left to give him a team-high 21 points.

"I was really on him last year all the time to shoot the ball," said Roy Williams, who coached his 200th game at UNC.

"I thought he was a big-time shooter and just didn't look for it. I talked to him all season about 'Don't forget your outside shot.' He hasn't forgotten it, thank goodness, this year."

Lawson's 49.3 shooting percentage on 3-pointers this season would lead the league if he qualified for the rankings (he doesn't, because he hasn't made enough).

Still, the guy with the reputation for beating everyone to the basket finally seems to be sloughing off the myth that he can't swish from the outside.

"The way they stepped off me and I was open this game, that surprised me," Lawson said. "I think I'm a good shooter, and coach says so too. So I don't know why people do that." ■

— Robbi Pickeral

Heels hold off Pack

CHAPEL HILL — Some people pound punching bags when they're frustrated.

Tyler Hansbrough beats up on N.C. State.

Once again, North Carolina's big man dunked back from a single-digit effort with a huge game against the Wolfpack, this time scoring 27 points — 20 in the second half — to lead the third-ranked Tar Heels to a 89-80 victory at the Smith Center.

It marked another big bounce-back by the senior forward, who scored only eight points at Miami on Sunday. The last time he was held to single digits — eight points on Jan. 28 at Florida State — he took his irritation out on the Wolfpack, too, recording 31 points several days later.

"Usually after he has a single digit game, he comes back and goes off — he's real aggressive, and he keeps attacking, he gets to the free throw line, and usually he has a big game for us," said forward Danny Green, who chipped in 19 points. "Unfortunately for them, they had to be the team we played the next game.

The Tar Heels (24-2, 10-2 ACC) led by only three points at halftime, a result of the sharp shooting by N.C. state point guard Javier Gonzalez, who was 6-for-6 — and tied a career-high four 3-pointers — in the first half, when he scored 16 of his 18 points.

Carolina missed its first two shots of the second half, but Hansbrough's putback-plus-free-throw began a 16-5 deluge during which the Tar Heels didn't miss a shot.

"Honestly, I wasn't happy with my first-half performance," said Hansbrough, who also grabbed

seven rebounds and tied a career-high with four assists. " I got it in my mind I was going to play a lot better in the second half."

UNC led by as many as 19 points, and although State (14-10, 4-7) closed the gap by shooting 64.3 percent in the second half, it never really got close because UNC, led by Hansbrough, shot 62.5 percent.

And while Hansbrough was swishing back from a sub-par performance, another Tyler — Tyler Zeller — was returning after a 13-week absence. After sitting out 23 games because of a fractured left wrist, the freshman 7-footer checked in to a standing ovation with 8:28 left in the first half. He immediately had State's Ben McCauley (nine points) drive around him for a bucket, and then recorded a field goal and two fouls before he checked back out. He finished with two points and four personal fouls in eight minutes.

"I asked him if he had butterflies," said UNC coach Roy Williams, whose team has now won 10 straight. "I think it calmed him down a little bit to make the first basket that he had. The physicalness bothered him ... so that's something that you'd like freshmen to be able to play some of those other opponents other than just start out in the ACC. ... I felt good about getting him some time, and I think in the long term he will help us, and that will really help him."

Still, the real comeback belonged to Hansbrough, who didn't practice Monday and sat out of contact drills Tuesday after suffering several blows to the head during Sunday's victory.

He has now scored 90 points in his last three games against State, and coach Sidney Lowe sounded glad that he won't have to face the senior again (barring a match-up in the ACC Tournament). Whether the player is coming off a single-

digit game or not.

"I'd love to watch him on television in the NBA," Lowe said. "I don't mind seeing him, just with another jersey on." ∎

— Robbi Pickeral

ABOVE: UNC's Tyler Hansbrough (50) drives past N.C. State's Dennis Horner (31) for two of his game high 27 points. ROBERT WILLETT/ THE NEWS & OBSERVER

LEFT: UNC's Danny Green (14) slams in two during the first half of UNC's 89-80 victory over N.C. State. ETHAN HYMAN/THE NEWS & OBSERVER

OPPOSITE TOP: UNC's Ed Davis (32) blocks the shot of N.C. State's Ben Mc-Cauley (34) in the second half. ETHAN HYMAN/THE NEWS & OBSERVER

OPPOSITE BOTTOM: UNC's Danny Green (14) gets a high five from team-mate Wayne Ellington (22). ROBERT WILLETT/THE NEWS & OBSERVER

FOLLOWING: UNC's Tyler Hansbrough goes to slam in two after being fouled by N.C. State's Courtney Fells (4). ETHAN HYMAN/THE NEWS & OBSERVER

THE NEWS & OBSERVER

Sports

www.newsobserver.com/sports

KELLY HONORED
Ravenscroft's Ryan Kelly is selected for the McDonald's All American team. **PAGE 6C**

< CAROLINA OUTDOORS
Two fishermen with ties to the Triangle are competing in the Bassmaster Classic. **PAGES 7-8C**

AP poll: A-Rod takes a hit

Baseball fans don't want him in Hall of Fame

By BEN WALKER
THE ASSOCIATED PRESS

More than half of baseball fans surveyed say Alex Rodriguez shouldn't make the Hall of Fame after admitting that he used steroids. And as for the game's hallowed records? Those same fans seem to care less and less anyway.

An Associated Press-GfK poll released Wednesday also showed this: Fans are losing interest in the whole steroids issue.

With 553 home runs, Rodriguez is considered likely to break Barry Bonds' career record of 762. Five of the top 12 home run hitters in history — Bonds, Sammy Sosa, Mark McGwire, Rafael Palmeiro and Rodriguez — have been tainted by allegations of steroid use.

According to the poll, 62 percent of baseball fans now take the game's records less seriously for that reason. But what about their marks?

"You can't take the numbers away from the guys," Texas slugger Josh Hamilton said. Hamilton was suspended from baseball multiple times for illegal drug use but never for performance-enhancing substances, said Wednesday.

"Did it make them feel better? Absolutely. But you've still got to hit the ball, you've got to throw the ball and you've got to catch the ball. I'm not defending them, but they've still got to swing the bat."

As for Rodriguez, 52 percent said he should not be allowed into the Hall when he becomes eligible, five years after his final game. In an AP-AOL Sports poll in April 2006, 61 percent of fans said Bonds shouldn't go into the Hall.

Eric Scott, 32, of St. Louis, said the Yankees slugger "should be suspended."

"People who have set records recently, there should be some kind of notation they were doing these illegal drugs," he said.

"I don't feel sorry because they got paid millions of dollars. They knew it was wrong. I feel sorry for the people who work really hard and may not be an All-Star because they didn't use performance-enhancing drugs. That's who I feel sorry for."

Rodriguez admitted Feb. 9 that he used

SEE **POLL**, PAGE 3C

Alex Rodriguez has admitted using steroids during a three-year stretch while he played for the Rangers.
AP PHOTO BY MARY ALTAFFER

Jeter defends 'clean' players

By RONALD BLUM
THE ASSOCIATED PRESS

TAMPA, Fla. — Derek Jeter wants fans to remember the "clean" guys.

The New York Yankees captain sat in the first-base dugout after his team's first full-squad workout of the season Wednesday, expressed support for Alex Rodriguez and tried to get a message out that will prevent the public from viewing the entire sport as tainted.

"One thing that is irritating and it really upsets me a lot is when you hear everybody say, 'It was the steroid era. Everybody was doing it.' You know, that's not true. Everybody was not doing it," he said.

With all the focus on A-Rod and his news conference Tuesday, Jeter bristled at those who group all players together.

"I think it sends the wrong message to fans, to baseball fans; I think it sends the wrong message to kids, saying that everybody was doing it, because that's just not the truth," he said. "I understand there's a lot of people who are big-name players that have come out and allegedly done this and done that, but everybody wasn't doing it."

A-Rod was the last of 60-plus Yankees to take the field. Some of the 1,600 or so fans gathered under a near-cloudless sky at Steinbrenner Field cheered when they saw No. 13. Not a single boo or insult was heard.

NORTH CAROLINA 89, N.C. STATE 80

Heels hold off Pack

HANSBROUGH BOUNCES BACK FROM SUB-PAR PERFORMANCE WITH 27

North Carolina forward Tyler Hansbrough stretches for two of his 27 points against N.C. State on Wednesday night in the Smith Center.
STAFF PHOTO BY ROBERT WILLETT

UNC builds a comfortable second-half lead, but N.C. State battles back thanks to some accurate shooting.

By ROBBI PICKERAL
STAFF WRITER

CHAPEL HILL — Some people pound punching bags when they're frustrated. Tyler Hansbrough beats up on N.C. State.

Once again, North Carolina's big man roared back from a single-digit effort with a huge game against the Wolfpack, this time scoring 27 points — 20 in the second half — to lead the third-ranked Tar Heels to a 89-80 victory at the Smith Center on Wednesday night.

We've seen this before from the senior forward, who scored eight points at Miami on Sunday. The other time this season he was held to single digits — eight points on Jan. 28 at Florida State — he took it out on the Wolfpack, recording 31 points several days later.

"Usually after he has a single-digit game, he comes back and goes off — he's real aggressive, and he keeps attacking, he gets to the free-throw line and usually he has a big game for us," said forward Danny Green, who chipped in 19 points. "Unfortunately for them, they had to be the team we played the next game.

The Tar Heels (24-2, 10-2 ACC) led by just three points at halftime, in part because of some sharp shooting by N.C. state point guard Javier Gonzalez, who was 6-for-6 — and tied a career-high with four 3-pointers — in the first half, when he scored 16 of his 18 points.

Carolina missed its first two shots of the second half, but Hansbrough's put-back-plus free throw sequence sparked a 16-5 run, during which the Tar Heels didn't miss a shot.

"Honestly, I wasn't happy with my

first-half performance," said Hansbrough, who also grabbed seven rebounds and tied a career-high with four assists. "I got it in my mind I was going to play a lot better in the second half."

UNC led by as many as 19 points, and although State (14-10, 4-7) closed the gap by shooting 64.3 percent in the second half, it never really got close because UNC, led by Hansbrough, shot 62.5 percent.

And while Hansbrough was bouncing back from a sub-par performance, another Tyler — Tyler Zeller — was returning after a 13-week absence. After sitting out 23 games because of a fractured left wrist, the freshman 7-footer checked in to a standing ovation with 8:28 left in the first half. He immediately watched State's Ben McCauley (nine points) drive around him for a bucket and then recorded a field goal and two fouls before he checked back out. He finished with two points and four personal fouls in eight minutes.

"I asked him if he had butterflies," said UNC coach Roy Williams, whose team has now won 10 straight. "I think

SEE **UNC**, PAGE 4C

PHOTO GALLERIES
See images, a First Look and video from the game. newsobserver.com/multimedia

INSIDE
TOUGH GOING: N.C. State's defense comes unglued in the second half. **► 4C**

Pack may see better days

CHAPEL HILL — With any luck at all, N.C. State's basketball team will not have to confront North Carolina's Tyler Hansbrough again.

From the Wolfpack's perspective, only two words could sum up that prospect: good riddance.

The Tar Heels' All-American forward on Wednesday night thoroughly worked over the Wolfpack one last time — assuming there isn't a third game this season in the ACC Tournament.

Hansbrough finished with 27 points and four assists in the Heels' 89-80 victory. That made his career record against the Wolfpack

Caulton Tudor

8-1 and gave him 90 points in his final three games in the series.

N.C. State coach Sidney Lowe said he's looking forward to next watching Hansbrough in the NBA, but he was quick to point to playmaker Ty Lawson as the primary key to the Heels' success.

"Lawson's the guy who makes them go. He's their glue, I think," Lowe said.

Where glue is concerned, the Tar Heels are five deep and possibly more. Coach Roy Williams didn't get a great deal from subs Ed Davis and Bobby Frasor, but Tyler Zeller did return for eight minutes in his first game since November. The 7-foot freshman committed four fouls but hit a field goal and came up with three rebounds.

In theory, the game was the perfect time for Williams to bring back Zeller, who had been out with

a wrist injury. State big men Brandon Costner, Ben McCauley, Tracy Smith and Dennis Horner had played a large role in the resurrection of the Pack's season.

That foursome hardly bothered the Pack (14-10, 4-7 ACC), combining for 49 points and collectively outplaying the UNC frontcourt for stretches. It was enough to keep Lowe optimistic.

But yet again, the Heels (24-2, 10-2) had too much firepower for the Wolfpack to overcome.

It's a theme Wolfpack fans are long tired of hearing and seeing. But maybe, just maybe, the situation is changing. After all, Hansbrough can't play college ball next season, and Lawson likely will skip his senior year for an NBA career.

caulton.tudor@newsobserver.com or 919-829-8946

Ty Lawson slides through the N.C. State defense on the way to a 17-point performance for UNC.
STAFF PHOTO BY ETHAN HYMAN

Greivis defeat for Tar Heels

North Carolina vs. Maryland // L 88-85   February 21, 2009

COLLEGE PARK, Md. — Maryland junior Greivis Vasquez on Saturday became latest opposing guard to join North Carolina's 30-point club.

Eventually, it was bound to bite the third-ranked Tar Heels in the loss column, again.

Vasquez's triple-double — 35 points, 11 rebounds, 10 assists — combined with UNC's poor shooting, questionable decision-making and poor composure down the stretch — resulted in a 16-point Maryland comeback and 88-85 overtime loss at Comcast Center.

Although Carolina (24-3, 10-3 ACC) remains atop the league standings with three games left in the regular season, Vasquez's historic performance yet again beamed a spotlight on a disturbing Tar Heels trend: poor perimeter defense.

The junior is the fourth guard to shred UNC for 30 or more points this season, joining Wake Forest's Jeff Teague (34), Florida State's Toney Douglas (32) and Miami's Jack McClinton (35). UNC is 2-2 in those contests (and in its other loss, Boston College guard Tyrese Rice scored 25).

"Greivis had a heckuva a game," UNC shooting guard Wayne Ellington said. "He made shots, got his team going. On the other hand, we were just flat out there. We were playing selfish; we weren't playing as a team."

That showed on the final stat sheet in many ways, from UNC's season-low five assists, to its 37.7 percent shooting, to point guard Ty Lawson's career-high 20 shots — a rather questionable number, considering all the talent around him — to the two turnovers in the final 98 seconds of regulation.

"The best team won today — the toughest team, the smartest team, the best-coached team won today," UNC coach Roy Williams said. "That's all I have to say."

Vasquez began his onslaught by scoring Maryland's first 16 points; but the junior — who was guarded in turn by Danny Green, Bobby Frasor and Lawson — went scoreless for the final 13 minutes of the first half.

Thus, UNC looked as if it would cruise to its 11th straight victory with 14:17 left in regulation, when a jumper by Green gave the Tar Heels a 52-36 lead. Then Vasquez started getting involved again, feeding assists to Cliff Tucker (22 points), hitting key buckets, using his long arms to frustrate Lawson on defense and helping his team end the second half with a 9-0 run.

With 9.2 seconds left in regulation, Vasquez's layup knotted the score 76-76.

With one second left, he blocked Lawson's jumper to send the game to an extra period.

With 1:16 left in overtime, he buried a go-ahead 3-pointer.

And with four seconds left in overtime — and his team leading by three — he helped force a turnover by Lawson, who slipped when the ball was inbounded to him.

"It was supposed to be me for a 3 or Wayne for a 3; it just didn't happen," said Lawson, who led UNC with 24 points.

Asked about the perimeter defense, Williams said his team hasn't played it as well as he has wanted all season, "and we didn't do it as well as we wanted to today."

And the question is, can it really improve? With UNC's best shutdown-man, senior Marcus Ginyard, out for the season because of a foot injury, the Tar Heels have no defensive stopper. And asked why guards keep scoring so much on them, players keep giving the same old excuse: they're just getting hot.

"Vasquez, he just causes match-up problems," Frasor said. "He's 6-6; he can get his shot off."

Again. And again. And again.

Vasquez's performance marked a career high, just like two of the three others who joined the Tar Heel 30-point club this season. He sounded proud to be part of the group.

"I talk to myself a lot and say 'I'm a good player' and I watch all those guys from other teams like Jack [McClinton] and Tyrese Rice, and I say 'When is the time when I'm going to have the game of my life?' " said Vasquez, whose triple-double was the third in Maryland (17-9, 6-6) history. "I just said 'You have to keep working and it will come.' It came at a great, great time, beating UNC and getting a triple-double. Hopefully, I have another one of those again." ∎

— Robbi Pickeral

ABOVE: UNC's Ed Davis (32) leaves the court after the Tar Heels are defeated by Maryland. ROBERT WILLETT/THE NEWS & OBSERVER

LEFT: UNC's Bobby Fraser fouls Maryland's Eric Hayes (5) with 11 seconds to play in overtime.
ROBERT WILLETT/THE NEWS & OBSERVER

FAR LEFT: UNC's Ty Lawson (5) drives to the basket against Maryland's Greivis Vasquez (21). ROBERT WILLETT/ THE NEWS & OBSERVER

OPPOSITE: Maryland's Greivis Vasquez (21) and Dino Gregory (33) double team UNC's Tyler Hansbrough (50).
ROBERT WILLETT/THE NEWS & OBSERVER

Heels pass their passing test

North Carolina vs. Georgia Tech // W 104-74   February 28, 2009

CHAPEL HILL — North Carolina was already leading Georgia Tech by 21 points Saturday when forward Tyler Hansbrough scored on a baseline jumper — after the seventh pass on that possession.

Guess last week's emphasis on sharing the ball sunk in.

Fourth-ranked UNC recorded 26 assists during its 104-74 blowout at the Smith Center, far better than the measly five assists it managed during its overtime loss at Maryland seven days before.

Hansbrough, in particular, benefitted from the extra passes. The senior All-American, who scored 28 points and ripped down 10 rebounds, broke the NCAA record for career free throws made. Wake Forest's Dickie Hemric swished 905 during a career that lasted from 1952-55. Hansbrough now has 907.

"It's an honor," said Hansbrough, who makes 50 free throws before practice each day as part of his routine. "But it's also a lot of fouls and a lot of hard work. It shows you have a good free-throw percentage, so it's good to be up there."

The victory — and the record — appeared to be a satisfying reward after last weekend's late-game meltdown at Maryland, which Hansbrough called "one of the most frustrating games of my career."

The senior said the ensuing practices were among the toughest he's experienced under coach Roy Williams — defensive drill after defensive drill, mixed in with extra sprints. But the coaches also harped on sharing the ball. The five assists against the Terps were the least by a UNC team since five in a 1997 game against Princeton.

In retrospect, the players said they were playing too much one-on-one and missing too many shots. At Maryland, 16 shots came after one or no pass, a real no-no in the Tar Heels' attack.

"We emphasized the 16 really, really, really bad shots that we took up at Maryland, but we emphasized the whole ballgame, and we had very complete practices," said Williams, whose team (25-3, 11-3 ACC) secured its third straight 25-win season.

Point guard Ty Lawson was key to Carolina's ball-sharing turnaround, tying a career record with 11 assists.

"I told him in the locker room that may be as good as I've ever seen a point guard play when he didn't have a field goal," Williams said.

Lawson, an ACC Player of the Year candidate who finished with four points on 0-for-3 shooting from the field, said he was trying to get his teammates more involved. But he insisted he wasn't trying to scale back his offense after taking a career-high 20 shots against the Terps.

"The opportunities weren't there," Lawson said. "Tyler, he was more open in the post, and it was an early game — and I'm not used to early games."

While Lawson may have needed a java jolt because of the noon tipoff, Hansbrough was as energetic as ever from the outset. Lawson and Frasor assisted him on six of his first 11 points, setting the tone for the rest of the game.

"I wish we could have denied him the ball a little bit more," lamented Tech coach Paul Hewitt, whose team (10-17, 1-13) has lost seven straight. "But he's a great player; what are you going to say?"

Meanwhile, Hansbrough's record-setting free throws came with 4:54 left, and he earned a standing ovation after his NCAA mark was announced during a later timeout.

Then the Tar Heels went back to ball-sharing mode. The big man's final field goal — the one after his team passed it around seven times — gave the Tar Heels an 82-59 lead.

The team-high 22 points from Tech's Lewis Clinch couldn't make a dent, especially with UNC's Danny Green scoring 18 of his 23 points in the second half.

"There were no rules," Green when asked if UNC had to make a certain number of passes before shooting. "Just get the shot we want. We know what's a good shot, we know what's not a good shot ... and we just worked for the good shot." ■

— Robbi Pickeral

LEFT: UNC's Tyler Hansbrough (50) shoots over Georgia Tech's Zack Peacock (35) in the second half. ROBERT WILLETT/THE NEWS & OBSERVER

OPPOSITE: UNC fans cheer for a free throw against Duke at the Dean Smith Center in Chapel Hill. CHUCK LIDDY/THE NEWS & OBSERVER

Seniors leave in style; Tar heels rally to beat Blue Devils and win ACC regular-season championship

CHAPEL HILL — After every big victory this basketball season, North Carolina's seniors tempered the accomplishment with the reminder that there's still more to do.

Yet Sunday, after beating seventh-ranked Duke 79-71 in their regular-season finale, they could finally take a moment to appreciate all they have done – so far.

By topping the Blue Devils for the sixth time in their four-year careers, Tyler Hansbrough, Danny Green, Bobby Frasor and Mike Copeland won their third regular-season ACC title — and second outright — enabling them to cut down the nets at the Smith Center once again.

That gives the second-ranked Tar Heels (27-3, 13-3 ACC) the top seed in this week's league tournament for the third straight season (they'll play the winner of Thursday's Virginia Tech-Miami game at noon on Friday). It also likely earned them a No. 1 seed in the NCAA Tournament for the third straight time as well.

All after starting the conference season 0-2.

"I think it's very important for seniors to go out on a good note and have a good memory going on their home floor," said Green, who played in his 116th victory, the most of any Tar Heel. "... And to go out with a winning record against Duke, that's a great feeling."

UNC coach Roy Williams said he always puts pressure on his underclassmen to make sure the seniors do, indeed, go out the "right way." Doing that against the Blue Devils (25-6, 11-5) looked like a challenge, though, considering Duke

ABOVE: Duke's Elliot Williams (20) gets hammered by North Carolina's Deon Thompson (21) as Danny Green (14) looks on in the second half.
CHUCK LIDDY/THE NEWS & OBSERVER

RIGHT: UNC senior Tyler Hansbrough (50) waves to fans upon his introduction, on "Senior Day," playing his final game in the Smith Center.
ROBERT WILLETT/THE NEWS & OBSERVER

had won five straight games and the Tar Heels' starting point guard, Ty Lawson, was questionable to play after jamming his right big toe on Friday.

In the end, Lawson (13 points, nine assists, eight rebounds) and fellow juniors Wayne Ellington (16 points) and Deon Thompson (14 points, including a key three-point play in the final minutes) did their parts. They helped their team shoot 52.8 percent for the game while cracking down on Duke's early sharpshooting in the second half (32 percent).

But many of the key moments came from the Tar Heel seniors, too:

• With 17:45 left, Green buried his first 3-point basket of the game, giving Carolina a 43-41 advantage. Duke cut it to a field goal on several occasions, but UNC led the rest of the way — in part because of another Green 3-pointer, with 3:13 left, that gave the Tar Heels a five-

LEFT: UNC fans (left to right) Niles Miller, Elias Clark and Billy Beaver cheer as the Tar Heels enter the Smith Center for their game against Duke. Robert Willett/The News & Observer

BELOW: UNC's Ty Lawson (5) drives against Duke's Kyle Singler (12). ROBERT WILLETT/THE NEWS & OBSERVER

point cushion. He finished with a dozen points.

• With 55 seconds left — just after Lawson made a three-point play to give the Tar Heels a 76-69 lead — Frasor made a key steal, thwarting Duke's final comeback attempt. He also made a 3-pointer in the first half, only his second connection from behind the arc since the last time the Tar Heels played Duke.

• And Hansbrough, as usual, was a dominant force in the lane, leading his team with 17 points and eight rebounds before he fouled out for only the third time in his career. Six of those points came on 3-pointers, another fun memory.

"Winning was important to me for the simple reason that it's my last time playing here," said Hansbrough, who has already qualified to have his No. 50 jersey retired. "And you always want to beat Duke ... and win the ACC; that's important, too."

Blue Devils coach Mike Krzyzewski said his team — which got 24 points from Jon Scheyer and 23 from Kyle Singler — played better defense, had better shots and competed better than when it lost to UNC on Feb. 11.

"But they're really good," Krzyzewski said of Carolina. "You know, if they're not the top team, they've got to be one of the top two or three."

Mostly because of the seniors, a rebuilding block class that finished with a 57-8 record in at home. The seniors said they would enjoy their latest accomplishment until midnight — and then refocus on trying to achieve more.

"It'll be back to business," Green said. "In practice, we'll keep pushing each other. ... We know what we're capable of doing, and hopefully we'll continue to do that." ∎

— Robbi Pickeral

Heels survive against Hokies; Hansbrough takes charge in clutch

ATLANTA — The prevailing theory entering Friday's first quarterfinal ACC Tournament game was that it didn't really matter to top-seeded North Carolina. Not with point guard Ty Lawson sidelined with a jammed right big toe. Not with a No. 1 seed in the NCAA Tournament all but a certainty. Not with a veteran cast of players who have won league titles before — and whose goal is a bigger championship.

But the Tar Heels shattered that supposition with the three little words that will be rewritten on the locker room white board again today, when they play fourth-seeded Florida State at 1:30 p.m.: "Find a way!"

"Our attitude is win every game possible, and win every tournament we can possibly win — no matter who's on the floor," senior Danny Green said after the Tar Heels (28-3) held off eighth-seeded Virginia Tech 79-76 at the Georgia Dome. "It's always going to go in the win or loss column, and we want it to go in the win column."

They put Friday in the win column using the same qualities they will have to repeat today, if they want to keep advancing without Lawson: stellar play by forward Tyler Hansbrough, solid performances by backup point guards Bobby Frasor and Larry Drew II, and some key moments off the bench by Justin Watts, Ed Davis and Tyler Zeller.

"We had a lot of people step up," said Hansbrough, who led the team with 28 points and was so excited afterward that he ran off the court through the wrong tunnel. "... If [Ty] can't go [today], we'll just have to have other players step up again."

Indeed, while Hansbrough "found a way" to seal the victory by tying up Hokies (18-14) forward J.T. Thompson in the lane with 5.2 seconds left, resulting in a turnover, several teammates found a way to put him in a position to do so:

• Frasor, an injury-plagued senior making just his third start since being the Tar Heels' top ballhandler his freshman season, played a career-high 36 minutes. He finished with just four points and three assists, but he committed only one turnover. His conditioning and lack of mistakes will be keys again today if the Tar Heels want to advance to their third straight league championship game.

"I'll hopefully get off my feet, rest, maybe ice some stuff down, take a hot and cold bath," Frasor said. "... But I feel good right now; maybe that's just adrenaline, but hopefully I feel good tomorrow."

• Drew II dished out as many assists (four) as he has his last four appearances combined, proving in 14 minutes that he's been honing his skills by facing the speedy Lawson each day.

"I do feel that Larry will give us more good things [today]," coach Roy Williams said. "It was a tough game for a freshman in his first ACC Tournament game. I'm sure he felt some pressures at times, but he did do some good things."

• And then there was the little-used Watts, perhaps the least likely

ABOVE: UNC's Tyler Hansbrough (50) muscles his way to the basket against Virginia Tech's Cheick Diakite (34) for two in the first half. ROBERT WILLETT/THE NEWS & OBSERVER

LEFT: UNC coach Roy Williams grabs the ball and reacts to a Tar Heel turnover in the second half during the ACC Tournament. ROBERT WILLETT/ THE NEWS & OBSERVER

OPPOSITE TOP: UNC's Danny Green (14) tries to move the ball against Virginia Tech forward Terrell Bell (1) in the first half of action at the ACC Tournament. CHUCK LIDDY/THE NEWS & OBSERVER

OPPOSITE BOTTOM: UNC's Tyler Hansbrough (50) gets his hands on the ball, and teammates Bobby Frasor (4) and Ed Davis (32) trap Virginia Tech's J.T. Thompson (33) as he tries to put up a shot. ROBERT WILLETT/ THE NEWS & OBSERVER

of the freshmen to be playing in the first-half of a postseason game. With Danny Green (2-for-13, five points) in foul trouble and the Tar Heels thin on perimeter players, the guard from Durham played five fairly-clean minutes before halftime, missing a shot but handing out an assist. The Tar Heels outscored the Hokies 13-11 when he was in the game; and he epitomized the determination to "find a way" to help.

"Coach told me to be ready, because he might need to call on me, and to just go out there and 'do what I tell you to do,' and that's what I did," Watts said.

Junior Wayne Ellington chipped in 16 points for the Tar Heels, while Davis added 10 and forward Deon Thompson 12.

A.D. Vassallo had 26 points and 10 rebounds for the Hokies.

Lawson — who was icing his foot while eating a sandwich after the game — is doubtful again to play against the Seminoles today, although a final decision won't be made until this morning.

With or without him, his teammates insist that contrary to the prevailing theory, they do want to prevail.

"We want to win it just as much as any other game," Ellington insisted. "We don't want to come in here and not play our hardest and not play our best, and say 'We don't care.' That's not our mind-set; that's not the type of team we are. Our next game, we'll be out there playing the hardest we can to try to win." ◼

— Robbi Pickeral

RIGHT: Noah Page, 8, along with his parents D.L. and Rhonda, from White Lake, cheer on the Tar Heels as they warm up. ETHAN HYMAN/ THE NEWS & OBSERVER

FOLLOWING LEFT: UNC's Tyler Hansbrough (50) finds the going tough inside against Florida State center Solomon Alabi (32) and Uche Echefu (41) during first half action in the ACC semi-final game. CHUCK LIDDY/ THE NEWS & OBSERVER

FOLLOWING RIGHT: UNC's Ed Davis (32) goes up against Florida State's Ryan Reid (42) in the first half. ROBERT WILLETT/THE NEWS & OBSERVER

BELOW: ACC player of the year, UNC's Ty Lawson (5), wears a special shoe with his uniform during team warm-ups. Lawson sat out the game with an injured big toe. ROBERT WILLETT/ THE NEWS & OBSERVER

Seminoles too much for Heels

North Carolina vs. ¹⁶Florida State // L 73-70   March 14, 2009

ATLANTA — As Danny Green's last-gasp, 3-point attempt to tie the score missed Saturday afternoon at the Georgia Dome, the truth emerged for top-seeded North Carolina: The Tar Heels might be able to win one tournament game with a player hurt and another hurting offensively. However it's very difficult to win two.

"I just couldn't find my groove," said a disappointed Green, who made only 1 of 12 field-goal attempts in UNC's 73-70 ACC Tournament loss to Florida State. The day before, Green shot 2-for-13 in the quarterfinals. "But hopefully, I find my touch soon."

Clearly, UNC must hope it's a matter of days and not weeks.

Point guard Ty Lawson, who sat out his second straight game Saturday because of a jammed right big toe, said he'll be healthy enough to start when his team begins NCAA Tournament play, likely as a No. 1 seed in Greensboro on Thursday. But the Tar Heels (28-4) are going to need all the firepower they can muster as Lawson gets back up to speed.

Against No. 4 seed FSU (25-

8), the Tar Heels got plenty from guard Wayne Ellington, who made 8 of 17 shots for a team-best 24 points. Then there was forward Tyler Hansbrough, who grabbed 11 rebounds to pass Sam Perkins for the school's career record and scored 22 points to put him three points shy of breaking Duke guard J.J. Redick's ACC career scoring mark.

But without Lawson — who buried a running 3-pointer to beat the Seminoles 80-77 in February — Carolina didn't have enough to counter FSU guard Toney Douglas' 27 points, or the Seminoles' 66.7 percent shooting in the second half.

"What made the difference was that we got the stops during the period of time that we had to get

the shots," said FSU coach Leonard Hamilton, whose team will play third-seeded Duke in the ACC title game today. "That's what has happened so much in the ACC. The games are in doubt down to the last three or four minutes, and the team that normally makes the plays at the end of the game pulls it out."

Indeed, Green, whose only field goal came on a tip-in to make it 8-8 in the first half, notched his only other points with 2:03 left in the game when he tied it 69-69 on two free throws.

After FSU's Derwin Kitchen gave his team a 73-70 cushion on two free throws with 15.1 seconds remaining, the senior forward had one more shot at redemption when Ellington missed a 3-pointer. Green snagged the loose ball, turned around, and put it up from beyond the arc.

"It was quickly rushed, but I thought it did have a chance," said Green, who finished with a season-low four points. "And I was hoping that it was going to go in, that all the shots that I missed yesterday and today wouldn't matter because I got the shot that we needed."

Instead, he said he'll be spending extra time in the gym over the next few days, trying to get the timing back on his layups and tip-shots, as well as the swish on his jumpers.

One plus in his favor: He has coach Roy Williams' vote of confidence.

"I think that you make your own momentum once you get in the tournament as a team, and I think you also make your own momentum as an individual," Williams said. "Whatever happened today should not have any effect on tomorrow. You have to be tough enough mentally to handle that."

Green said he has that mental fortitude and has shown it in the

past. When he shot 3-for-13 at Miami on January 17, he followed that performance by making eight of his 12 shots against N.C. State. When he went 2-for-10 at Virginia Tech earlier this month, he converted half of his shots the next game against Duke.

Green hasn't posted back-to-back shooting performances this poor all season, and he's determined that the skid ends in Atlanta. With Lawson on the mend, Green said he wants his team to have its full range of firepower for the NCAA Tournament.

"I'm disappointed with how I played, but I know I can do better," he said. "... Our season is not over." ∎

— Robbi Pickeral

LEFT: UNC's Roy Williams watches during the second half of UNC's 73-70 loss to Florida State in the semifinals of the ACC. ETHAN HYMAN/THE NEWS & OBSERVER

OPPOSITE: Florida State's Toney Douglas (23) breaks free from the pressure of UNC's Bobby Frasor, right, and Deon Thompson during the second half. ETHAN HYMAN/THE NEWS & OBSERVER

NCAA Tournament 1st Round: Radford

March 19, 2009

Heels stomp Radford; Tyler Hansbrough becomes the ACC's all-time leading scorer as North Carolina eases into the second round

North Carolina vs. Radford // W 101-58   **March 19, 2009**

GREENSBORO — It came with the swish of a free throw, the first of two with 15:43 left in Thursday's first half, sending the baby-blue clad crowd to its feet for a raucous ovation.

Tyler Hansbrough took a moment to appreciate breaking the ACC's all-time career scoring mark, and then the focused North Carolina forward returned to making sure he and the Tar Heels didn't make another sort of history.

In the end, UNC easily avoided becoming the first regional top seed to ever fall to a No. 16 in NCAA Tournament. Even with point guard Ty Lawson missing his third straight game because of a jammed right big toe, North Carolina routed Radford 101-58 at the

Greensboro Coliseum.

Because of the sharpshooting of Wayne Ellington (25 points), a career-high from freshman forward Ed Davis (15 points) and the typical production of Hansbrough (22 points) in the lane, Carolina (29-4) will play eighth-seeded LSU on Saturday at 5:45 p.m. in the second round.

And it was the way Hansbrough celebrated his feat — by calmly swishing his second free throw, with little show of emotion — that showed yet again how determined he is to have a bigger celebration after winning five more games and the national title.

"Once I got the standing ovation, I thought about waving — but no disrespect to anybody, I just wanted to stay focused on the game," he said.

It has been that way since the start of the season, when fans and media started calculating how many games it would take him to surpass

former Duke guard J.J. Redick's 2,769 points.

The date was delayed because of an early season shin injury, which sidelined him for four games. Then it was pushed back again by a couple of rare single-digit performances — at Florida State and at Miami.

"It does kind of feel like it was a long time coming," said Hansbrough, who also had five rebounds in 20 minutes. "It is great to get it over with. I'm just glad I don't have to talk about it forever, or think about it or listen to everybody who's got the little point tracker and whatever."

Those point trackers kept ticking for the first 4 minutes, 17 seconds, when Hansbrough missed his first two shots of the game, made his third and was fouled hard by Highlanders forward Phillip Martin while going up for a shot in the lane.

UNC led 11-9 at the time and 13-9 afterward.

For the final 30 minutes of the game, the Tar Heels never led by fewer than 10 points.

"I'm just glad Tyler broke the record on a free throw; that's pretty fitting," teammate Bobby Frasor said.

An NCAA record 953 of Hansbrough's career's 2,789 points have come at the line. And although he

RIGHT: Bradley Buchner, 7, (left) and Griffin Link, 8, both of Asheville, show their support for the Tar Heels with signs they constructed from recycled cardboard, and markers from Bradley's mom's purse. ROBERT WILLETT/ THE NEWS & OBSERVER

FAR RIGHT: UNC's Tyler Hansbrough (50) walks through a sea of fans as he enters the court for practice on Wednesday, March 18, 2009, in the Greensboro Coliseum. ROBERT WILLETT/ THE NEWS & OBSERVER

PREVIOUS: Alyssa Prete, 15, and her mom, Mary Beth Powell, 52, cheer on the Tar Heels late in the second half against Radford. CHUCK LIDDY/ THE NEWS & OBSERVER

missed 11 of his 16 shots from the field Thursday, he was 12-for-12 from the line.

"He's the best," said Radford center Art Parakhouski (10 points, 10 rebounds), one of four Highlanders (21-12) to finish in double figures. "I knew he was the best in the nation, and I'm expecting him to play like he did today. I just tried to compare with him, but I didn't bring my best game today, and I missed a lot of shots due to the [pace of the] game, you know."

After the final buzzer, Hansbrough was given the game ball in the locker room — which he promptly handed off to team officials to place in the Carolina basketball museum, where a pile of his trophies and other memorabilia will soon reside.

He was told that Redick, now with the NBA's Orlando Magic, had asked for his phone number and was planning to call to offer congratulations.

He reiterated that he appreciated the reaction of the fans, and that the record "is a big deal to me," even if it didn't show on his face at the line when he set it.

"When you think of the players in this league and the caliber of the players and understand that he scored more points than anybody that's played here, that's as big as it can be," UNC coach Roy Williams said. "But as he said, he was trying to focus on winning a game."

And now, a championship. ∎
— Robbi Pickeral

RIGHT: Radford's Phillip Martin (30) fouls UNC's Tyler Hansbrough (50) sending him to the free-throw line, where Hansbrough would set the ACC scoring record for most points.
ROBERT WILLETT/THE NEWS & OBSERVER

Sports
www.newsobserver.com/sports

TOURNAMENT TIME
Stephen Curry scores 32 as Davidson knocks South Carolina out of the NIT. **PAGE 4C**

< PLAY-IN WINNER
Morehead State will take on Louisville in the first round of NCAA play. **PAGE 4C**

Captain plans on staying

Brind'Amour not ready to step away

BY CHIP ALEXANDER
STAFF WRITER

RALEIGH – Rod Brind'Amour of the Carolina Hurricanes is in his 20th year in the NHL and will play his 1,394th game tonight against the New Jersey Devils.

As Canes coach Paul Maurice put it, "That's a lot of miles."

But while 20 years in hockey can take its toll, while this season has had its ups and downs, Brind'Amour says there will be a 21st, that he hasn't given any thought to retirement.

"It's not a question of whether I'm going to play again," Brind'Amour said. "I know I still love the game, and I still think I can play. And that's the key."

For Brind'Amour, this season has been more trying and taxing than any of the 19 before it. There were times he appeared slower than usual on the ice, when he couldn't quite make plays, lost key faceoffs, turned the puck over.

It was after those plays, those games, that one had to wonder if at 38, and coming off major knee surgery last year, Brind'Amour's best hockey was behind him. A former Selke Trophy winner as the league's best defensive forward, his plus/minus rating drifted into uncharted — for him — territory.

"But 20 years in the league — he's seen it all," the Canes' Sergei Samsonov said. "He knows how to deal with everything."

When the coaching staff pulled Brind'Amour off a West Coast road trip after a Feb. 3 game in Vancouver and sent the team captain back to Raleigh to rest and treat a groin injury, Brind'Amour dealt with it. When Maurice reduced his playing time, he dealt with it. No public outbursts, no sulking.

"I don't think he was playing as poorly as he was accused of, and I do think he was hurting," Maurice said. "It just got to the point he needed to rest his body.

"We all know he's a good, solid player. But he would never come out and excuse his play on anything that most every other player would and say, 'I'm banged up or this isn't going well or the coach isn't using me right.' "

In the 17 games before he was sent back to Raleigh, Brind'Amour did not score a goal, had five

SEE **HURRICANES,** PAGE 6C

HURRICANES' PLAYOFF CHASE

11
Games remaining

WHERE THEY STAND
The Canes (79) hold eighth place in the Eastern Conference, two points behind the seventh-place Montreal Canadiens and one ahead of the Florida Panthers.

NEXT GAME

NEW JERSEY AT CAROLINA
7 p.m. today, RBC Center, Raleigh
TV: FSCR **RADIO:** WCMC-99.9

Lawson's big toe still a big concern

NO WORD ON WHETHER THE JUNIOR POINT GUARD WILL PLAY THURSDAY

ACC Player of the Year Ty Lawson, right, is crucial to North Carolina's chances of winning the national title.
STAFF PHOTO BY ROBERT WILLETT

Ty Lawson is taking a ribbing from some of his teammates about his lingering toe injury, but it's no laughing matter for North Carolina basketball coach Roy Williams.

BY ROBBI PICKERAL
STAFF WRITER

CHAPEL HILL – Because of all the angst, questions and speculation about Ty Lawson's lingering limp, North Carolina shooting guard Wayne Ellington can't help but tease his teammate.

"I say, 'Man, there's nothing wrong with you — you've got a jammed toe,'" Ellington said Tuesday, grinning.

As trivial as the injury seems, however, it has become no joke.

Tar Heels coach Roy Williams reiterated that he doesn't know whether Lawson, the ACC Player of the Year, will play Thursday in Greensboro when the top-seeded (South Region) Tar

STAFF ILLUSTRATION BY TIM LEE

Heels face No. 16-seeded Radford in the first round of the NCAA Tournament. Williams said the junior point guard would need to practice Tuesday and today in order to return. (The school gave no update on Lawson after Tuesday's workout.)

"Maybe it's wishful thinking, but I really expected it to respond quicker than it has," Williams said. "And after he had played against Duke, I didn't really expect that much swelling to happen — that's what really set everything backward. I guess I've been a little surprised at the severity of it. I've just been thinking it every day, 'It's going to get better, it's going to get better,' but I'm probably as discouraged right now at this moment as I have

SEE **LAWSON,** PAGE 4C

LIVE CHAT
Does J.P. Giglio really think North Dakota State will upset Kansas? Talk online with ACC Now's resident expert about the NCAA Tournament today at 1 p.m. Go to newsobserver.com and click on the "NCAA live chat" banner.

LIVE UPDATES
Our NCAA Tournament team will be in Greensboro today posting updates from North Carolina's and Duke's practice sessions for their opening-round games Thursday. Go to blogs.newsobserver.com/accnow

---

Scheyer natural leader

Desire to succeed developed early

BY KEN TYSIAC
STAFF WRITER

DURHAM - Four years ago, Jon Scheyer's mother called his high school coach one Saturday morning with some unusual news.

"Jon is going crazy," coach Dave Weber said Laury Scheyer told him. "He's writing a letter to every kid on the team."

Glenbrook North, Scheyer's high school, had completed its regular season the night before and was heading into the playoffs. Scheyer wanted to win a state title and was leaving nothing to chance.

He typed out individual letters to each teammate, instructing them on the roles they needed to play for the school to win a championship.

He wanted Zach Kelley to rebound and score inside.

Scheyer's backcourt partner, Sean Wallis, needed to be a leader and hit shots. Scheyer told Malik Valliani he needed to become a good passer.

"His leadership is incredible," Weber said. "You can talk about it, but it was so natural with him. He just did it."

That's why it seems so natural to Weber that Scheyer is thriving at Duke after being moved from shooting guard to the starting point guard spot on Feb. 19. The point guard is supposed to be the leader and steadying force for a team, and Weber said that role fits Scheyer perfectly.

With Scheyer claiming most outstanding player honors at the ACC Tournament, Duke seized the league title Sunday at the four-day event.

Before his move to the point, Scheyer was averaging 13.1 points a game. Since the move, he has averaged 20.2 points in nine games. Eight of those games have been wins for Duke (28-6), which will meet Binghamton (23-8) in a first-round NCAA Tournament game at about 9:40 p.m. Thursday in Greensboro.

"I like having the ball in my hands," Scheyer said Tuesday. "I feel like I'm not going to make

SEE **DUKE,** PAGE 4C

UNC VS. RADFORD

WHEN: Approximately 2:50 p.m. Thursday
WHERE: At Greensboro Coliseum
TV: WRAL, WNCT

DUKE VS. BINGHAMTON

WHEN: Approximately 9:40 p.m. Thursday
WHERE: At Greensboro Coliseum
TV: WRAL, WNCT

WAKE VS. CLEVELAND ST.

WHEN: Approximately 9:40 p.m. Friday
WHERE: At American Airlines Arena, Miami
TV: WRAL, WNCT

NCAA Tournament 2nd Round: LSU

March 21, 2009

Lawson lifts Heels

North Carolina vs. ²¹LSU // W 84-70   **March 21, 2009**

GREENSBORO — North Carolina point guard Ty Lawson's jammed big toe hurt every time he dribbled right, slid on defense or pivoted.

But he also knew the alternative would have been much more painful.

With his top-seeded team's NCAA Tournament life on the line at Greensboro Coliseum, the junior returned from a three-game absence to score a gutsy 23 points — all but two in the second half — to lead his team past eighth-seeded LSU 84-70.

The Tar Heels (30-4) advanced to play Gonzaga on Friday in Memphis in the round of 16. It will mark UNC's 23rd trip to the NCAA regional semifinals.

"It was the first time coach has ever called me a 'tough player,' or anything like that," said Lawson, who first started having his threshold for pain questioned last season, when he missed seven games for two different ankle injuries.

"I wanted to show everybody that I am a tough player, that I can play through an injury — and that satisfied me, knowing I could show everybody that."

He looked less than 100 percent early, missing his first three shots. But the ACC Player of the Year showed his intestinal fortitude when, with his team leading 17-12 with about 11:30 left in the first half, he pushed off his taped right toe on defense and heard it pop —

sending him to the bench and his team into a short tailspin.

While the trainer was treating him — "he said I probably just popped some of the scar tissue, which I was trying to get rid of anyways, so hopefully it was a good thing," Lawson said — LSU reeled off an 8-2 run to take a 20-19 lead.

With Lawson back in the game, and Wayne Ellington scoring 11 of his 23 points before the break, Tar Heels led 38-29 at halftime.

But the aggressive Tigers began the second period with a 13-3 surge that included six points from Tasmin Mitchell, two blocks on Tyler Hansbrough (who didn't score a second-half field goal until 4:48 remained) and a timeout by UNC coach Roy Williams, who asked one simple question: "Do you want your season to end right now?"

Lawson, looking like his old speedy self by the minute, immediately answered with his second 3-pointer of the half tie the score 44-44 with 15:54 left.

Then, again, seven minutes later.

A 3-pointer by Tigers wing Marcus Thornton tied it 63-63 with 8:35 remaining. But UNC countered with a 17-2 run — including an athletic three-point play, a jumper and two free throws by Lawson; and Danny Green's only 3-pointer of the game — to pull away for good.

"That and one [Ty] had, I didn't think he was going to be strong enough or tough enough to bull his way up, but that was an incredible play," senior guard Bobby Frasor said. "... Ty is a special player, and I'm glad he's back."

Now the question is, is he back for good? Lawson iced his toe — which he injured when he collided with a basket support in practice

on March 6 — immediately after the game. But as dozens of reporters crowded around him during the postgame media session, he said that he could feel it swelling.

Still, he said he didn't expect it to react as badly as it did when he played on the hurt toe during the March 8 game at Duke, because he planned to treat it differently.

"That was probably our fault," Lawson said. "My dad, he was like, 'Put it in hot water Epsom salt.' It's an old remedy, old school, so I was like, 'All right, I'll try it.' But then it swelled up real big, and I told the doctors, and they just looked at me like I was crazy. I won't do that again — I'll just ice it from now on."

Thornton led LSU with 25 points; Tasmin Mitchell added 18.

"We just let one slip away," Thornton said.

Mostly because they let Lawson — who also handed out six assists with no turnovers — slip by, despite his achy toe.

"Sometimes he does limp around and act soft, but I know how tough he can be," Green said. "When the game's on the line, big-time players step up and do big-time things. I knew he was going to step up and do some things for us." ∎

— Robbi Pickeral

LEFT: North Carolina forward Tyler Hansbrough (50) contests a second half shot by LSU guard Marcus Thornton (5). CHUCK LIDDY/ THE NEWS & OBSERVER

OPPOSITE: North Carolina guard Ty Lawson (5) tries to keep the handle on the ball against the defense of LSU guard Bo Spencer (11). CHUCK LIDDY/ THE NEWS & OBSERVER

PREVIOUS: The Tar Heels huddle together after player introductions for their game against LSU. ROBERT WILLETT/THE NEWS & OBSERVER

RIGHT: UNC's Ty Lawson (5) drives to the basket against LSU's Bo Spencer (11) in the first half. Lawson led the Tar Heels with 23 points. ROBERT WILLETT/ THE NEWS & OBSERVER

OPPOSITE: North Carolina guard Ty Lawson (5) checks his toes after a mid-court collision in the first half. Lawson was out for a few minutes in obvious pain but re-entered the game. CHUCK LIDDY/THE NEWS & OBSERVER

FOLLOWING LEFT: North Carolina guard Ty Lawson (5) drives the base-line in the second half. CHUCK LIDDY/ THE NEWS & OBSERVER

FOLLOWING RIGHT: UNC coach Roy Williams tells his players to play tough defense after breaking the game open with a 72-63 lead over LSU in the second half. ROBERT WILLETT/ THE NEWS & OBSERVER

Ellington can't miss at right time

North Carolina vs. LSU // W 84-70   March 21, 2009

GREENSBORO — No doubt about it, center stage belonged to Ty Lawson in North Carolina's 84-70 second-round win over Louisiana State on Saturday night in Greensboro Coliseum.

But again, it was the marksman on the wings, Wayne Ellington, that the Tar Heels could not have survived without.

With Lawson still slowed by an angry right big toe in the first half, and Tyler Hansbrough held basically in check by the Tigers defense in the second, Ellington carried the offense through stretches and played one of the best overall games of his career.

"I just tried to keep moving and make plays," Ellington said. "We knew LSU was going to be tough, and that we'd have to respond. From the start, I just wanted to make plays whether I was making shots or not."

He did both, finishing with 23 points by going 7-for-13 with two 3-pointers and 7-for-7 on free throws, plus four assists, two steals, a blocked shot and instrumental hustle plays on both ends against LSU (27-8), which posed a bigger problem that the final score suggested.

The win sends Carolina (30-4) to the South Regional semifinals on Friday in Memphis, where the opponent will be Gonzaga.

Beale Street, B.B. King blues tunes, the Peabody Hotel lobby and big platters of barbecue ribs appeared to be a million miles away after the Tigers went up 54-49 with 12:23 left.

That was when Ellington turned into Wellington at Waterloo, scoring a breakaway after forcing a turnover, bagging a mean 3-pointer and feeding teammate Ed Davis for a bucket to ignite a seven-point run that put the Heels back ahead 56-54.

"That was a key time in the game," Carolina coach Roy Williams said. "But really, Wayne gave us such a big lift all game. He did a lot more than shoot, too. Like he said, he just made a lot of things happen for us in other areas."

No surprise there. Dating to a win over Duke to end regular season on March 8, the 6-foot-4 Ellington's jump shot has been almost automatic, including 24 points against Florida State in an ACC Tournament loss and a 25-point outburst in Thursday's first-round NCAA victory over Radford.

Radford's one thing. Doing it against LSU defensive terror Garrett Temple (6-6, 195 pounds) was something entirely different.

"He was incredible out there," teammate Danny Green said. "Every time we needed a big play, he came up with one."

At halftime, when the Heels had a seemingly comfortable 38-29 edge, Hansbrough had 12 points and Ellington 11, Lawson was struggling with two points and four misses on his five shots.

Lawson exploded in the second half to finish with 23 points and the usual zero turnovers for the game. Hansbrough got off to a slow start after halftime and was limited to three points during the final 20 minutes, but Ellington more than covered the shortage.

Looking ahead, the Heels couldn't ask for a much better hand, assuming Lawson can play on without interruption:

• Hansbrough's not going to held to 15 often.

• Green's shooting touch is still off, but hey, he was a perfect 1-for-1 on left-handed attempts against the Tigers. He's still working the boards and hustling on defense.

• Sixth man Ed Davis is playing more like the junior he'll likely never be than a freshman.

• Bobby Frasor is doing a lot of little things, including playing solid defense.

• And Ellington is on the hot streak of a lifetime. ∎

— Caulton Tudor

Sweet 16: Gonzaga

March 27, 2009

Lawson leads way; UNC point guard scores 17 in first half, sets up second-half push

North Carolina vs. [10]Gonzaga // W 98-77   March 27, 2009

MEMPHIS — Throughout the ACC basketball season, North Carolina point guard Ty Lawson had been content to be a second-half offensive force — preferring to get his teammates involved early and then doing his own scoring later on.

But on Friday night, he flipped his approach — and flicked Gonzaga out of the NCAA Tournament at FedExForum.

With a trip to the South Regional final on the line, the junior scored 17 of his 19 points before halftime, giving the top-seeded Tar Heels a big enough cushion to withstand a second-half Bulldogs run and make their 98-77 victory look downright easy at times.

As a result, Carolina (31-4) will play second-seeded Oklahoma at 5:05 p.m. on Sunday for a chance to advance to the Final Four. The Zags (28-6) were making their 11th straight trip to the NCAA Tournament and fifth appearance in the regional semifinals.

"They gave me open 3s, so I just knocked them down and got everything rolling," Lawson said. "I started pump-faking, getting to the basket, shooting, getting fouled. They just gave me opportunities to score, so I did."

On Thursday, Lawson had said his jammed right big toe felt like a 6 on a scale of 1 to 10.

It's hard to imagine what he might have done had it been a 7 or 8.

The speedy junior, who had scored 124 of his 159 points during the second halves of his previous seven games, was aggressive from the outset, taking advantage of the Bulldogs' zone defense. He buried two early 3-pointers that gave his team a 15-9 lead. A jumper followed by a transition bucket gave his team a 35-25 advantage and a third 3-pointer made it 38-27.

And it didn't help the Zags that their own speedy point guard, Jeremy Pargo, picked up his third foul just 13 minutes into the game. Or that starters Austin Daye and Matt Bouldin combined to make only 6 of their 18 shots.

Carolina led by as much as 49-32 in the first half, when shooting guard Wayne Ellington — who continued his sizzling shooting streak with 19 points — buried a free throw with about four minutes left in the first half. The Tar Heels took a 53-42 advantage into halftime.

"Usually, we don't get into the half with a spread like that," Danny Green said. "[Ty's] points ... really

RIGHT: UNC's Tyler Hansbrough (50) tangles with Gonzaga's Matt Bouldin (15) for an offensive rebound in the first half. ROBERT WILLETT/THE NEWS & OBSERVER

PREVIOUS: UNC coach Roy Williams congratulates Tyler Hansbrough (50) after a crowd-pleasing dunk during the Tar Heels' practice on Thursday, March 26, 2009. ROBERT WILLETT/THE NEWS & OBSERVER

OPPOSITE: UNC's Wayne Ellington (22) drives to the basket past Gonzaga's Ira Brown (50) for two of his 19 points. ROBERT WILLETT/THE NEWS & OBSERVER

helped make that happen."

And unlike against LSU, the Tar Heels didn't let up.

Lawson, who had scored 59 percent of his points in second halves (295-of-500) this season, scored to give his team a 57-42 cushion early in the second half. Then, with the Zags' defense shading toward him, Lawson started to get his teammates more involved.

After Green (13 points) buried his second 3-pointer of the game — the first time he has made more than one in a game since March 8 — Lawson fed Ellington a transition layup with 15:01 left that gave the Tar Heels their first 20-plus-point cushion (66-45).

Gonzaga countered with a run of its own — as one would expect from a round-of-16 team — outscoring the Tar Heels 12-2 to cut the lead to 68-57.

But reserve guard Bobby Frasor hit back-to-back 3-pointers, then Ellington scored on a 3-point play, to keep the Heels out of trouble.

With 9:10 left, Lawson checked out of the game and took off his left shoe at the end of the bench; but the minor injury was on the opposite foot of his injured toe.

"I rolled my left ankle a little bit because I put so much pressure on my left foot," Lawson explained. "I did the same thing during the LSU game, but it's not that bad — it wasn't the toe at all."

And with 6:52 left, his shoe was back on and he was back in the game, dishing out his ninth and final assist, to Green on another 3-pointer that made it 90-66.

Hansbrough led all scorers with a workmanlike 24 points, plus 10 rebounds.

"It was good for [Lawson] to get that toe warm, to get his shot falling, get to the basket, get and-ones — do everything he's done all year," Frasor said. "I think he probably came out wanting to test the toe right away, and scoring like that in the first half — that just shows that he can do it any time, anywhere. He's not just a second-half player." ∎

— Robbi Pickeral

ABOVE: UNC's Ty Lawson, center, takes a seat on the bench after scoring 19 points against Gonzaga.
ROBERT WILLETT/THE NEWS & OBSERVER

OPPOSITE LEFT: UNC's Tyler Hansbrough (50) smiles as he watches the final two minutes of the second half. Hansbrough led UNC with 24 points. ROBERT WILLETT/ THE NEWS & OBSERVER

OPPOSITE RIGHT: UNC's Danny Green (14) shoots over Gonzaga's Austin Daye (5) in the second half. ROBERT WILLETT/THE NEWS & OBSERVER

Elite 8: Oklahoma

March 29, 2009

Lawson in UNC's playmaking pantheon

North Carolina vs. ⁷Oklahoma // W 72-60   March 29, 2009

MEMPHIS — Entering Sunday's NCAA South Regional championship game, North Carolina's Ty Lawson had a modest personal goal.

"When I leave," the junior playmaker said Saturday, "I'd like to be remembered as one of the top point guards at Carolina. One of the top five, I'd say. If I'd get in that group, that would be in some great players."

If Lawson wasn't already there, which he was of course, there's no debate now. The question, after he led the Tar Heels to a 72-60 win over Oklahoma and the school's 18th

Final Four trip, is exactly how far up the point guard pecking order does Lawson belong?

Phil Ford, from the mid-'70s, is generally regarded as the grand high alpha of that fraternity. Raymond Felton in 2005 directed his team to an NCAA championship. So did Tommy Kearns in 1957 and Derrick Phelps in 1993. Jimmy Black was at the controls when the Heels won in 1982 and reached the championship game in '81.

But going back all the way to Kearns and that undefeated '57 team, it's

difficult to find a Carolina playmaker more instrumental to his team's success than Lawson has been this season. It was never more apparent than Sunday in the FedExForum, where he was voted regional most outstanding player after burying with the Sooners with his 19 points, five rebounds, five assists and three steals against one turnover.

"He was incredible. He makes them go," Oklahoma coach Jeff Capel said. "He's almost impossible to contain."

Lawson had support, of course. Teammates Danny Green (18 points, nasty perimeter defense) and Wayne Ellington (nine points, three rebounds) helped Carolina (32-4) dominate the perimeter and transition.

But on a day when Oklahoma's interior defense limited Tyler Hansbrough to eight points and the Soon-

ers' Blake Griffin piled up 23 points and 16 rebounds, Lawson drove his team to Detroit's Ford Field Final Four and a shot at East champ Villanova (30-7) in Saturday's semifinal nightcap at about 9 p.m. Michigan State (30-6) and Connecticut (31-4) will begin the Final Four at 6:07.

From UNC coach Roy Williams straight down the bench, Lawson's performance was praised — sensational, great, spectacular and maybe the most complimentary of all, "predictable."

"I just tried to be a leader," Lawson said. "Everybody on this team can be a star, though. It takes all of us."

Nothing Lawson did came as a great shock, of course.

En route to the ACC player of the year award, he was led the rescue squad each time the Tar Heels

encountered danger. When he was sidelined by a late-season toe injury, the team struggled to escape Virginia Tech and then lost to Florida State in the ACC Tournament. Upon his return against LSU in second-round NCAA game in Greensboro, Carolina again resumed the look of the nation's best team.

"Ty believed [in this team], and he caught a lot of criticism when we were 0-2 in the league and he had been through a tough time against [Boston College's] Tyrese Rice and [Wake Forest's] Jeff Teague," Williams said. "But Ty doesn't have to take a backseat to anyone. He's still Dennis the Menace some of the time, but he's been just terrific."

It was after those two early season losses that Lawson literally accelerated into the league's best point guard. Against Villanova, he'll have to deal with speedsters Scottie Reynolds and Corey Fisher.

But how do you take anyone against Lawson at this point? There isn't a hotter playmaker, or player, in the country. And if Lawson surprises almost everyone by returning for a fourth season, Phil Ford himself might have to surrender his territory. ■

— Caulton Tudor

LEFT: UNC's Deon Thompson (21) puts up a shot over Oklahoma's Blake Griffin (23). ROBERT WILLETT/ THE NEWS & OBSERVER

OPPOSITE LEFT: UNC's Ty Lawson (5) drives past Oklahoma's Austin Johnson (20). ROBERT WILLETT/ THE NEWS & OBSERVER

OPPOSITE RIGHT: UNC's Ty Lawson (5) leads a fast break in the first half ahead of Oklahoma's Blake Griffin (23). ROBERT WILLETT/THE NEWS & OBSERVER

PREVIOUS: UNC's Tyler Hansbrough (50) wears his piece of the net after the Tar Heels' 72-60 victory over Oklahoma. ROBERT WILLETT/THE NEWS & OBSERVER

MONDAY, MARCH 30, 2009 — THE NEWS & OBSERVER — F ■ ■ ■ ■ C +

Sports
www.newsobserver.com/sports

HELPING CHILDREN
Former N.C. State players Torry and Terrence Holt are in town for a special event. **PAGE 2C**

 HE'S BAAAAAAACK!
With a big back-nine rally, Tiger Woods takes his first win since undergoing surgery. **PAGE 3C**

Seniors show off tonight

Women's teams go for Final Four spot

BY EDWARD G. ROBINSON III
STAFF WRITER

RALEIGH – Maryland and Louisville meet tonight at the RBC Center with a women's Final Four berth on the line.

On the line, too, are the reputations of three of the nation's top seniors, who enter the game with outside expectations of dynamic, high-scoring, game-altering performances.

Kristi Toliver and Marissa Coleman lead the top-seeded Terrapins (31-4) against Angel McCoughtry and the third-seeded Cardinals (32-4) in the Raleigh Regional final. The winner advances to the NCAA Tournament semifinals in St. Louis.

Toliver, Coleman and McCoughtry have shown — throughout their careers and this tournament — they can dominate a game and will their team to victory. Each has scored more than 2,000 career points and made

SEE **RALEIGH**, PAGE 7C

Angel McCoughtry averages 23.3 points, 9.1 rebounds for the Cardinals.
STAFF PHOTO BY ETHAN HYMAN

TODAY'S GAME

RALEIGH REGIONAL CHAMPIONSHIP
NO. 1 MARYLAND WOMEN VS. NO. 3 LOUISVILLE
WHEN: 7 p.m.
WHERE: RBC Center, Raleigh
TV: ESPN
RECORDS: Louisville 32-4, Maryland 31-4
TICKETS: $20 adult, $15 student/youth, 919-865-1510, www.gopack.com

INSIDE
MORE NCAA ACTION: Connecticut women remain undefeated. ▸ 6C

Johnson stays in control at Martinsville

BY DAVID POOLE
STAFF WRITER

MARTINSVILLE, Va. – Jimmie Johnson and Denny Hamlin found a way to disagree without being disagreeable after the Goody's 500 at Martinsville Speedway.

Johnson said the move that led to his victory in Sunday's Sprint Cup race was not a bump-and-run. Johnson, who won for the fifth time in the past six races at its .526-mile track, contended it was Hamlin who initiated the contact that sent Hamlin's No. 11 Toyota up the track in Turn 4 and allowed Johnson to take the lead.

"It was time to go," Johnson said after posting his 41st career victory. "It was just good, hard racing. He was just trying to protect his lead, and I wanted to win, too."

Hamlin said he didn't feel that he

TOP FIVE
1. J. Johnson
2. Denny Hamlin
3. Tony Stewart
4. Jeff Gordon
5. Clint Bowyer

SEE **RACE**, PAGE 8C

NORTH CAROLINA 72, OKLAHOMA 60

Motown bound

TAR HEELS USE THEIR DEPTH TO EARN A RETURN TRIP TO THE FINAL FOUR

BY ROBBI PICKERAL
STAFF WRITER

MEMPHIS, Tenn. – When North Carolina forward Tyler Hansbrough climbed the ladder at FedExForum on Sunday night, snipped his segment of the net and raised a celebratory fist to the cheering Tar Heels fans, one thing became apparent:

It doesn't matter whether he's the best player in the country. Because once again, he plays for a Final Four team.

Despite watching their star senior get outdueled by Oklahoma star sophomore Blake Griffin, the Tar Heels dominated the Sooners 72-60 with their depth, defense and dynamic point guard Ty Lawson.

As a result, they will play Villanova, the East Region winner, at approximately 8:47 p.m. Saturday in Detroit for the right to advance to the national title game. It marks UNC's 18th trip to the Final Four, equaling UCLA's record number of appearances (although the Bruins' 1980 trip was later vacated by the NCAA).

"It felt great to get up there and cut down the net again," said Hansbrough, who still bristles at the bitter memory of losing in the national semifinals last season. "I've felt a lot of pressure — and I just felt relief. There's been a lot of expectations on this team — and for me, it feels good to be

SEE **UNC**, PAGE 4C

UNC's Ty Lawson, who scored 15 of his 19 points in the second half, earned most outstanding player honors in the regional.
STAFF PHOTOS BY ROBERT WILLETT

AS ACC. All the time

SUNDAY'S RESULTS
ROUND OF EIGHT

No. 1 North Carolina	72
No. 2 Oklahoma	60
No. 2 Michigan State	64
No. 1 Louisville	52

FINAL FOUR
AT FORD FIELD, DETROIT

NO. 2 MICHIGAN STATE (30-6) VS. NO. 1 CONNECTICUT (31-4)
6:07 P.M. SATURDAY (WRAL, WNCT)

NO. 1 NORTH CAROLINA (32-4) VS. NO. 3 VILLANOVA (30-7)
8:47 P.M. SATURDAY (WRAL, WNCT)

INSIDE
BRACKET: The updated NCAA Tournament bracket. ▸ 5C
NOVA NIPS PITT: Scottie Reynolds hits winning shot. ▸ 8C

YOUR BRACKETS
See how your brackets are doing at ncaa.newsobserver.com, and vote for your favorite talking heads on hoops in the Battle of the Broadcasters at share.triangle.com/ncaa.

PHOTO GALLERIES
 See more images and a First Look from the UNC-Oklahoma game.

LIVE UPDATES
Follow the Final Four with updates from N&O writer Robbi Pickeral at blogs.newsobserver.com/accnow.

Lawson in UNC's playmaking pantheon

MEMPHIS – Entering Sunday's NCAA South Regional championship game, North Carolina's Ty Lawson had a modest personal goal.

"When I leave," the junior playmaker said Saturday, "I'd like to be remembered as one of the top point guards at Carolina. One of the top five, I'd say. If I'd get in that group, that would be in some great players."

If Lawson wasn't already there, which he was of course, there's no debate now. The question, after he led the Tar Heels to a 72-60 win over Oklahoma and the school's 18th Final Four trip, is exactly how far up the point guard pecking order does Lawson belong?

Phil Ford, from the mid-'70s, is generally regarded as the grand high alpha of that fraternity. Raymond Felton in 2005 directed his team to an NCAA championship. So did Tommy Kearns in 1957 and Derrick Phelps in 1993. Jimmy Black was at the controls when the Heels won in 1982 and reached the championship game in '81.

But going back all the way to Kearns and that undefeated '57 team, it's difficult to find a Carolina playmaker more instrumental to his team's

SEE **TUDOR**, PAGE 4C

Caulton Tudor

Forward Danny Green, right, embraces Deon Thompson after UNC's regional final victory over Oklahoma.

Seth Curry decides to join the Blue Devils

BY RON GREEN JR.
STAFF WRITER

Seth Curry has found his new basketball home, and Duke coach Mike Krzyzewski has found a future scorer.

After spending several hours Sunday with Krzyzewski on the Duke campus, Curry — the nation's leading freshman scorer (20.3 points per game) this season at Liberty — committed to play for the Blue Devils.

Under NCAA rules, Curry will not be allowed to participate next season but can begin play in

Seth Curry is headed to Duke.

the 2010-11 season.

After spending five hours with Coach K and his staff and hearing how highly they regard [Seth] and how they think he can help their program, it speaks for itself," father Dell Curry said Sunday evening. "It seems like the right fit. Seth committed before he left."

Curry, the younger brother of Davidson star Stephen Curry, asked for and was granted his release from Liberty to pursue what he called "opportunities at higher-rated conferences."

Curry's father said after Liberty had granted his son's release, the school was contacted by Duke officials about meeting with the 6-foot-3 Charlotte Christian graduate.

"They did everything right by the book," said Dell Curry, a former Virginia Tech and Charlotte Hornets star. "When [Duke] requested to talk with Seth, they jumped to the top of the list."

Curry said his son had planned to visit other schools until he met with Krzyzewski and his staff Sunday.

"Coach K really wanted Seth," Dell Curry said. "His vision for Seth and for the program — it was great as parents to hear someone of his stature sell us on how bad he wanted Seth."

Krzyzewski is not allowed to comment on Curry until he signs with the school.

With Seth's future determined, there is still a question about whether his older brother will return to Davidson for his senior season or turn professional.

Dell Curry said he and his wife, Sonya, talked with Stephen on Friday and Saturday about his decision, but nothing has been finalized.

Staff writer Tom Sorensen contributed to this report.

rgreenjr@charlotteobserver.com or 704-358-5118

ABOVE: UNC fans, from left, Christy Bray, Anna Holland, Mark Reidy and kara Fujita watch UNC's win over Oklahoma at Top of the Hill, a popular bar in Chapel Hill. TAKAAKI IWABU/ THE NEWS & OBSERVER

LEFT: The UNC bench celebrates an early first half lead over Oklahoma. ROBERT WILLETT/THE NEWS & OBSERVER

OPPOSITE: UNC senior Danny Green (14) glides to the basket over Oklahoma's Juan Pattillo (12). ROBERT WILLETT/ THE NEWS & OBSERVER

RIGHT: UNC's Tyler Hansbrough (50) drives against Oklahoma's Blake Griffin (23) in the second half. ROBERT WILLETT/ THE NEWS & OBSERVER

OPPOSITE: UNC's Tyler Hansbrough (50) gets tangled with Oklahoma's Blake Griffin (23). ROBERT WILLETT/ THE NEWS & OBSERVER

FOLLOWING TOP: UNC coach Roy Williams and his team celebrate their 72-60 victory over Oklahoma. ROBERT WILLETT/THE NEWS & OBSERVER

FOLLOWING BOTTOM: Coach Roy Williams cuts down the net in the FedEx Forum in Memphis, as the Tar Heels celebrate their victory over Oklahoma, clinching the South Regional and securing a trip to the Final Four. ROBERT WILLETT/THE NEWS & OBSERVER

FOLLOWING RIGHT: UNC coach Roy Williams and his team celebrate. ROBERT WILLETT/THE NEWS & OBSERVER

Final Four: Villanova

April 4, 2009

Heels take final step; Junior guard Wayne Ellington scores 20 points against his hometown school

North Carolina vs. [11]Villanova // W 83-69   April 4, 2009

DETROIT — Had junior guard Wayne Ellington wanted to stay close to home, play in the Big East, be the obvious superstar on an up-and-coming team, he would have chosen Villanova.

But he picked North Carolina because he wanted to play for a national championship. And now, thanks to his team's 83-69 victory over the Wildcats on Saturday night in the NCAA semifinals, that's exactly what he will do.

Ellington scored 20 points on 7-for-14 shooting over his No. 2 college choice at Ford Field. It wasn't the most among his star-studded teammates, but it didn't have to be.

To earn a national title date Monday night against Michigan State — the very team it blew out by 35 points in December — UNC also needed a 22-point performance from point guard Ty Lawson; a typically tough output from forward Tyler Hansbrough (18 points, 11 rebounds) and some well-timed shots by wing Danny Green (12 points).

It will mark UNC's second trip to the NCAA championship game in the past four years. The Tar Heels won their fourth NCAA title in 2005.

"It feels so great," said Ellington, who also pulled down nine rebounds. "We worked so hard in the offseason and all year long to be able to play in this big game. Now, we will."

Before the starting lineups were announced, the showdown opened with a montage of the five Tar Heels starters asking, "Remember us? We're baa-aack." And from the beginning, they looked as if they meant to stay.

There were a couple of early bobbles — Hansbrough's two missed free throws to open the game stand out — before Ellington buried a baseline jumper to make it 2-2.

But unlike last April, when they

seemed happy just to make it to the Final Four showed in the way Kansas ripped off a 40-12 game-opening run, the Tar Heels were both poised and efficient from the outset.

Leading 10-8, UNC (33-4) padded its cushion with a 16-4 run, during which five different players scored, to take a 26-12 lead on Ellington's second 3-pointer of the game. During that stretch, it was the Wildcats — making their first Final Four appearance since 1985 — who looked like the wobbly newcomers, missing shot after shot.

It was an early sign of what was to come, as Nova made just 32.9 percent of its shots for the game.

The Wildcats (30-8) didn't roll over, though. With Carolina leading 47-31 with about four minutes left in the half, the Wildcats used a 9-2 run — including five points by Scottie Reynolds, who led his team with 17, to trim their deficit to 49-40 at the break.

They further whittled UNC's lead to 50-45 early in the second half, thanks to a 3-pointer by Reggie Redding and a jumper by Shane Clark.

But with memories of last year's national semifinal disappointment lingering in their heads, the Tar Heels used two 3-pointers from Green and a transition bucket by Lawson — who had to change briefly into jersey No. 25, after some of Hansbrough's blood stained his No. 5 — to rebuild their dominance.

"It did get a little tense," senior guard Bobby Frasor said. "But Danny, just like he has done all year, hit a big 3, and Ty got that and-1, and that got us back up to 10 right there."

Ellington's fourth 3-pointer with 6:56 left gave the Tar Heels a 70-55 cushion.

Then his fifth 3-pointer with 4:46 left gave Carolina a 75-57 advantage.

"I felt like I was in the gym, working

out in the summer time against these guys back home," Ellington said of his shooting touch. "It was a lot of fun."

It was an ugly second half, as neither team shot better than 31 percent.

And Carolina was far from perfect, missing 15 free throws for the game and getting outrebounded on the offensive boards by eight.

But with so much firepower and talent, it didn't matter. That's what drew Ellington to Chapel Hill. And now, that's what gives the sharpshooter the ultimate bragging rights over Villanova starters Clark and Redding (15 points), who are from Philadelphia and remain close friends.

Because he's going to play for a national championship. And they are not.

"It was real competitive; there wasn't any trash-talk or anything like that," Ellington said. "It was just good fun basketball." ∎

— Robbi Pickeral

LEFT: Villanova's Scottie Reynolds (1) can't move the ball inside against North Carolina's Danny Green (14) and Tyler Hansbrough (50). ROBERT WILLETT/ THE NEWS & OBSERVER

OPPOSITE: North Carolina's Wayne Ellington (22) cradles the ball as time runs out on Villanova and UNC wins. ROBERT WILLETT/THE NEWS & OBSERVER

PREVIOUS: UNC's Ty Lawson (5) drives to the basket, slicing through the Villanova defense in the second half. Lawson, who was fouled on the play, led all scorers with 22 points. ROBERT WILLETT/THE NEWS & OBSERVER

FOLLOWING: UNC's Ty Lawson (5) plays keep away with Villanova's Corey Fisher (10) in the first half. ROBERT WILLETT/THE NEWS & OBSERVER

Final Four

SPORTS INSIDE

HURRICANES CLINCH PLAYOFF BERTH

Anton Babchuk's goal at 1:11 of overtime beats the visiting Penguins 3-2. **PAGE 5C**

NORTH CAROLINA 83, VILLANOVA 69

Heels take final step

FUELED BY A STRONG FIRST HALF, UNC MOTORS INTO MONDAY'S NCAA CHAMPIONSHIP GAME

North Carolina point guard Ty Lawson jets downcourt after making a steal during the first half against Villanova. Lawson, who led the Tar Heels with 22 points, scored on the play.
STAFF PHOTOS BY CHUCK LIDDY

It's a championship or bust for Carolina

Caulton Tudor

DETROIT — It's always been about the whole shebang for this North Carolina basketball team. That's remained the overriding theme — a daily swig of motivation — since the Tar Heels left San Antonio empty-handed, wet-eyed and

roundly panned after last season's Final Four.

The quest for vindication in 2009 now goes to the final fling — a date with Michigan State (31-6) of the Big Ten in Monday's national championship game at 9:07 p.m. at Ford Field.

Carolina (33-4) reached the title game with an often ugly, sometimes bloody 83-69 win over Villanova (30-8) late Saturday, a

SEE TUDOR, PAGE 3C

ACCNOW
All ACC. All the time.

LIVE UPDATES

Follow the Final Four with updates from staff writers Robbi Pickeral, Caulton Tudor and Ken Tysiac at **blogs.newsobserver.com/accnow**.

PHOTO GALLERIES

Check out the action from the Final Four including First Look from the UNC-Villanova game at **newsobserver.com/sports**. You even can buy prints of your favorite photos.

INSIDE

ALL FOR ONE: Heels stay together, even for CBS. ► **3C**

Junior guard Wayne Ellington scores 20 points against his hometown school to help North Carolina move on to a showdown with Michigan State.

By ROBBI PICKERAL
STAFF WRITER

DETROIT — Had junior guard Wayne Ellington wanted to stay close to home, play in the Big East, be the obvious superstar on an up-and-coming team, he would have chosen Villanova.

But he picked North Carolina because he wanted to play for a national championship. And now, thanks to his team's 83-69 victory over the Wildcats on Saturday night in the NCAA semifinals, that's exactly what he will do.

CHAMPIONSHIP GAME

North Carolina vs. Michigan State
9:07 p.m., Monday, WRAL, WNCT

Ellington scored 20 points on 7-for-14 shooting over his No. 2 college choice at Ford Field. It wasn't the most among his star-studded teammates, but it didn't have to be.

To earn a national title date Monday night against Michigan State — the very team it

blew out by 35 points in December — UNC also needed a 22-point performance from point guard Ty Lawson, a typically tough output from forward Tyler Hansbrough (18 points, 11 rebounds) and some well-timed shots by wing Danny Green (12 points).

It will mark UNC's second trip to the NCAA championship game in the past five seasons. The Tar Heels won their fourth NCAA title in 2005.

SEE UNC, PAGE 3C

MICHIGAN STATE OR CONNECTICUT

It's a championship or bust for Carolina

North Carolina vs. [11]Villanova // W 83-69   April 4, 2009

It's always been about the whole shebang for this North Carolina basketball team.

That's remained the overriding theme — a daily swig of motivation — since the Tar Heels left San Antonio empty-handed, wet-eyed and roundly panned after last season's Final Four.

The quest for vindication in 2009 now goes to the final fling — a date with Michigan State (31-6) of the Big Ten in Monday's national championship game at 9:07 p.m. at Ford Field.

Carolina (33-4) reached the title game with an often ugly, sometimes bloody 83-69 win over Villanova

(30-8) late Saturday, a couple of hours after the Spartans eliminated four-point favorite and once No. 1-ranked Connecticut (31-5) in the semifinal opener 82-73.

Just like that, the Big East's big show was over.

While the ACC-based Tar Heels have been chasing the trophy since an 84-66 semifinal loss to Kansas exactly one year ago today, Michigan State didn't really emerge as a loud bracket crasher until doing away with the Jayhawks and top-ranked Louisville in the Midwest Regional final.

Tom Izzo's team now shows no signs of being inferior to the Tar

Heels, who were also ranked No. 1 during regular season, or anyone else. There's no question the game site is right up Michigan State's alley.

"We love Detroit. The best is yet to come," Spartans coach Tom Izzo said seconds after his team's win.

Those words were sweet Motown sounds to most of the 144,000 or so ears in the sold-out football stadium. It's the place Detroit's Lions have so thoroughly turned into a bottom-feeders football mansion that the city's sports fans were starving for a reason to cheer inside the building's gates.

While the Tar Heels, Connecticut and Villanova had decent representations in the stands, Ford Field this weekend has become a bulky version of Michigan State's Breslin Center.

Whether it was the unsightly elevated playing court, an acute case of Final Four jitters or the green-out

in the stands, Connecticut's players were uncomfortable and uncertain from the start. It was a weakness Izzo's players fed on early and then feasted on late.

Carolina hardly was the personification of poise and precision, either. Although the Heels were able to take big leads in both halves, the performance was well below those against Gonzaga and Oklahoma a week earlier in the South Regional at Memphis, Tenn.

After leading 40-23 with seven minutes left in the first half, Carolina playmaker Ty Lawson went into a rare stretch of errant free-throw shooting that seemed to spill over to everything his teammates touched.

A rash of turnovers, rushed shots and some dominant Villanova rebounding allowed the Wildcats to close the deficit to 50-45 a couple of minutes into the second half.

Fortunately for the Heels, their hectic ways were contagious. After drawing so close, Villanova reverted to bad shot selection and heavy fouling.

At some stage shortly before the 16:49 mark, a cut opened on Tyler Hansbrough's hand, blood from which found its way to Lawson's jersey, forcing him to switch from No. 5 to No. 25 for a brief period.

Seconds later, Carolina went on another spurt and moved back ahead 75-57 even as Hansbrough, benched by four fouls, watched.

So uneven was the game flow that UNC guard Wayne Ellington didn't

LEFT: UNC'S head coach Roy Williams ponders his team's play during the first half against Villanova.
ROBERT WILLETT/THE NEWS & OBSERVER

OPPOSITE: North Carolina's Danny Green (14) and Deon Thompson (21) battle Villanova's Shane Clark (20) and Dwayne Anderson (22) in the second half. ROBERT WILLETT/THE NEWS & OBSERVER

score for more than 13 minutes in the second after piling up 13 points in the first half. And Lawson, who clanked free throws left and right for a while, still finished with 22 points and eight assists.

Hansbrough, unusually intense even by his standards, overcame the foul difficulty to get 18 points and 11 rebounds. Ellington had 20 points plus nine rebounds.

"They're just better than us," Wildcats coach Jay Wright said.

"We were actually feeling pretty good at halftime when it was back to nine [49-40], but they did a lot of little things that didn't allow us to make the run we thought we could make. We didn't play our best game, but the No. 1 reason was the other team. They're that good."

But it was not classic Carolina hoops by any interpretation. Something better, certainly smoother, will be required Monday. ∎

— Caulton Tudor

"Getting Ty back was what we needed," Hansbrough said.

Something else regarding Hansbrough has changed, too. His critics seem to be multiplying the longer he hangs around. He's become boring to some, much like a guest lingering past bedtime.

The most frequent rap is that Hansbrough is all-shoot and no-stop.

That's true to a degree. Certainly, he's a better offensive player than defensive. So is almost every player in a Roy Williams program. The man has won 592 games in

21 seasons by emphasizing point production.

Hansbrough can't be blamed for becoming a prolific product of the system. Had he signed with, say, Wisconsin, some people today might be hailing his defense and passing but knocking his offense.

Lately, it's become popular to compare Hansbrough, last season's national player of the year, to the Sooners' Blake Griffin, this season's top player and likely No. 1 NBA pick. So what? Neither is in the NBA yet. Besides, the pro and col-

Tar Heels still need Psycho-T

April 4, 2009

DETROIT — Time was, North Carolina could not have won many games in which Tyler Hansbrough played only 26 minutes and scored no more than eight points.

Things have changed as one of the school's most decorated players ever nears the end of a four-year run.

In last week's South Regional final against Oklahoma, Hansbrough's 26 minutes, eight points and six rebounds weren't much more than contributing factors.

Not only did the team win, the score was 72-60. At one stage, Carolina led 61-40 as Hansbrough's presence changed from go-to man to roving decoy. In foul trouble early, he was swarmed by a defense that then couldn't check Ty Lawson and Danny Green outside.

Hansbrough was front-and-center during the celebration.

"I've never cared about who scores," he said. "I've said that a lot of times. As long as we score enough to win, I'll be the happiest person around."

Although right-shin pain in November made Hansbrough sit out early games, that injury did as much

to frame the season as last year's embarrassing Final Four loss to Kansas.

"Everyone else had to do more," Lawson said. "We had to learn to win games without him. It was tough, but that was the only choice we had."

Carolina won four games when Hansbrough couldn't help and two others when he played 25 minutes or less.

It was Lawson whom the Heels couldn't do without. When a late-season toe injury sent the junior playmaker to the sidelines, Carolina hit a full-blown crisis.

Had Lawson not recovered for NCAA games against Louisiana State, Gonzaga and Oklahoma, neither Hansbrough nor anyone else could have done enough to put the Heels opposite Villanova (30-7) today in this Final Four.

RIGHT: UNC's Tyler Hansbrough (50) drives to the basket against Villanova's Corey Fisher (10) in the second half. ROBERT WILLETT/THE NEWS & OBSERVER

OPPOSITE: North Carolina's Tyler Hansbrough (50) looks to move against Villanova's Shane Clark (20). ROBERT WILLETT/THE NEWS & OBSERVER

lege games are different.

A part of it is Hansbrough's appearance.

On his calmest day, he can come across as awkward and frantic, complete with the wide-eyed glare of someone who fights an endless war against contact lenses. He's lost a step of quickness, which he hardly had in abundance at the outset.

And while Hansbrough has been a solid athletic citizen, there's his personality. He doesn't give a hoot what people outside the program think about his playing style. He's going to bust a butt — his, yours, maybe both — to win. At game's end, there will no apology extended or expected.

"Most of the time, though, he's just this big kid who wants to have fun and enjoy life," teammate Bobby Frasor said. "People who don't like him don't know him."

That big kid's team role may have changed, but he hasn't. Whether you like Hansbrough or not, you have to admit Carolina wouldn't have been remotely as good without him.

The Tar Heels won't win this championship without a big parting gift from Hansbrough, either. Things haven't changed that much. ■

— Caulton Tudor

Cousy Award goes to Heels' Lawson; Junior chosen nation's top point guard

April 4, 2009

DETROIT — The NCAA Tournament semifinals won't tip off until Saturday, but North Carolina junior guard Ty Lawson's trip to the Final Four already has been productive.

He will receive his own hardware as the winner of the Bob Cousy Award, which has been given since 2004 to the nation's top point guard as selected by a blue-ribbon committee of Hall of Famers, sports information directors and media members.

After deciding to forgo the NBA draft and return to school, Lawson is averaging 16.3 points and 6.5 assists per game and will lead the Tar Heels (32-4) against Villanova (30-7) on Saturday. On Monday morning, the Basketball Hall of Fame will formally present Lawson with the Cousy Award for his performance this season.

Lawson is the second North Carolina point guard in four years to earn the award. Raymond Felton won it in 2005. Texas' D.J. Augustin, who now is a teammate of Felton's with the NBA's Charlotte Bobcats, won in 2008.

The award won't fatten Lawson's wallet as much as his initial night in town. Coach Roy Williams gave the team a 1:30 a.m. Thursday curfew, and Lawson cashed in. Lawson said he made $250 playing craps after the team arrived in Detroit on Wednesday night.

He doesn't have any more plans to gamble while he's in Detroit.

"It's probably the last time I'll go there before the games start," Lawson said during Thursday's media interview session.

North Carolina sports information director Steve Kirschner said Williams doesn't have a problem with Lawson gambling, because it's not illegal, and Lawson is of legal age. Playing craps is not against NCAA rules, which are limited to a ban on gambling on sporting events.

During a conference with the media, NCAA president Myles Brand was asked about athletes gambling at the Final Four.

"What a student does, plays bingo in his church, for example, while we discourage that, we prefer not to try and regulate that particular kind of activity," Brand said. "But it's highly discouraged."

HEELS, WILDCATS TRADE BARBS

The many close relationships between Villanova and North Carolina players have led to some friendly trash talk.

Villanova wing Dwayne Anderson said Lawson recently texted him with a message: "You know we're going to beat y'all, right?"

Anderson said he texted back: "You better get your ankles taped twice."

"Because of his foot injury, and all," Anderson explained.

Considering the distance between the campuses, the number of friendships between the teams' players is surprising. Lawson and Scottie Reynolds were roommates two summers ago as counselors at the LeBron James Skills Academy in Akron, Ohio.

North Carolina guard Wayne Ellington, who grew up near the Villanova campus in Philadelphia, has a lot of friends on the Wildcats team. Ellington said he's closest to Reggie Redding and Shane Clark.

Ellington attended Episcopal Academy near Philadelphia along with Villanova coach Jay Wright's children. He se-riously consid-ered the Wildcats before choosing North Carolina because of its tradition.

"I wanted a chance to be able to contend for a national championship," Ellington said. "Which sounds crazy now that Nova is in the Final Four. But back then, it was clear that Carolina was the decision to make if I wanted to contend for a national championship."

SPARTANS GETTING LOCAL LOVE

A giant green sign with a Spartans emblem on the Wayne County office building in downtown Detroit welcomes Michigan State to the Final Four in huge lettering.

In much smaller print, the sign mentions the other three Final Four participants — North Carolina, Connecticut and Villanova. There's no doubt who's the favorite in this town, and Michigan State players are embracing their status as champions of a city that's down on its luck with the auto industry struggling.

"We definitely can be an inspiration," said Michigan State sophomore guard Durell Summers, a Detroit native. "Guys can look at us and see what hard work can do, or what being the underdog and not giving up can do." ■

— Ken Tysiac

ABOVE: UNC senior Bobby Frasor (4) applauds his teammates' performance as he steps to the court for a time-out late in the second half against Villanova. ROBERT WILLETT/ THE NEWS & OBSERVER

RIGHT: UNC's Danny Green (14) goes to the basket against Villanova's Antonio Pefia (0) in the second half. Green scored 12 points. ROBERT WILLETT/ THE NEWS & OBSERVER

FAR RIGHT: The Carolina student section celebrates their 83-69 victory over Villanova. ROBERT WILLETT/ THE NEWS & OBSERVER

Championship: Michigan State

April 6, 2009

Not even close: UNC rolls to title

DETROIT — As he went down the bench, alternately pumping a fist and hugging his teammates with a minute left Monday night, you could see it all in North Carolina forward Tyler Hansbrough's expression:

The elation. The relief. The redemption.

No matter the outcome of Monday's game, Hansbrough — one of the most decorated players in school history — would have left UNC a winner. But by helping shellac Michigan State 89-72 at Ford Field, he finished his career with the ultimate emotion: the pride of being a national champion.

"Sounds like I made a pretty good decision," Hansbrough, freshly cut net around his neck, said of forgoing the NBA last summer and returning for his senior season. "Nothing beats this feeling right here."

Hansbrough contributed to UNC's fifth NCAA title in typically tough fashion: 18 points, seven rebounds. Yet it was point guard Ty Lawson who pushed the Tar Heels with 21 points and a title-game record eight steals; freshman forward Ed Davis who pulled them with a team-leading eight rebounds; and junior Wayne Ellington who was voted the most outstanding player of the Final Four after making seven of his 12 shots.

That seemed a fitting way to win it, because that's how Carolina (34-4) grew stronger the latter part of the season — with Hansbrough still starring but also allowing others to emerge.

Hansbrough and company took the boisterous green-clad crowd out of the game early, first when he won the opening jump ball on a redo, then by contributing five points during a 36-13 game-opening run. It served as a flashback of last April's national semifinal loss to Kansas but in reverse: Instead of the Tar Heels being on the tense end of a 40-12 dismantling, it was the Spartans who were feeling the pain of it all.

After the first 20 minutes, UNC led 55-34 — the most points scored in a half of an NCAA championship game and the biggest halftime lead in a title game. Hansbrough had 11 points, but Lawson dominated with seven steals — tying the NCAA record — while Ellington swished 17 points and Davis grabbed five rebounds.

And it didn't stop there.

MSU (31-7), which lost to UNC by 35 points here in December, just couldn't keep up with UNC's transition game or points in the paint.

Coach Tom Izzo — whose Spar-

tans had the hopes of an economically depressed city behind them — had predicted that if both teams played well, the Tar Heels would prevail. But although Goran Suton, who didn't play the last time the teams met, had 17 points and 11 rebounds, UNC played great.

With about 13 minutes left, Spartans reserve Durrell Summers scored on a layup to close the once-24-point gulf to 62-46. But UNC small forward Danny Green — as he has done all season — buried a clutch 3-pointer to calm any run attempt. With about 10 minutes left, MSU closed to 15 down, but Hansbrough scored on an inside move to make it 70-53.

And when Michigan State closed to 78-65, Lawson scored on a drive to put the game out of reach, again.

"Everybody talked about how we were a different Michigan State team, where for eight games we've been pretty good — but we were not that way today," Izzo said.
"... We couldn't stop Ellington outside, or Hansbrough inside, or Lawson getting to the line [where he was 15-for-18]."

Hansbrough, the ACC's all-time leading scorer, insisted this week he

LEFT: North Carolina's Ty Lawson (5) works the ball in against Michigan State's Durrell Summers (15) in the first half. CHUCK LIDDY/THE NEWS & OBSERVER

OPPOSITE LEFT: North Carolina's Tyler Hansbrough (50) shoots over Michigan State's Goran Suton (14) during the first half. ROBERT WILLETT/ THE NEWS & OBSERVER

OPPOSITE RIGHT: North Carolina's Ty Lawson (5) fires up the team after he is sent to the foul line in the first half against Michigan State. CHUCK LIDDY/ THE NEWS & OBSERVER

PREVIOUS: The Tar Heels burst onto the court after winning the NCAA men's championship game. CHUCK LIDDY/THE NEWS & OBSERVER

didn't necessarily need a national championship to secure his legacy. Not with dozens of school, league and NCAA records secured. Not with the 2008 consensus national player of the year trophies stuffed in a closet and four years' worth of All-American honors under his belt. Not with his No. 50 jersey already scheduled to be retired in the Smith Center rafters.

But ever since he was a kid practicing power moves on an 8-foot backyard basket, he dreamed about an NCAA title. So the chance to lead UNC to its fifth one is what drove him to put off the NBA for one last year, to deal with the escalating taunts and criticism from opposing fans and national media, to recover from an early-season shin injury, to get bruised and bloodied and booed for one more season.

And to ultimately heave the NCAA championship trophy.

In addition to winning it all, Hansbrough, Bobby Frasor, Green and Mike Copeland leave Carolina with a 124-22 record, making them the winningest class in Carolina's history — surpassing Quentin Thomas' 123-victory mark set last season.

Roy Williams also became only the 13th coach to guide his team to multiple NCAA titles.

"The first one in 2005 was sweet," Williams said, "but this one is even sweeter."

Just another reason for Hansbrough to circle the court, hugging everyone in sight, as the final horn of his final college game sounded.

"I'm just a part of something special right here," Hansbrough said. "It's the best feeling in the world." ■
— Robbi Pickeral

RIGHT: North Carolina's Tyler Hansbrough (50) and Michigan State's Travis Walton (5) do the second tip off to open action. CHUCK LIDDY/THE NEWS & OBSERVER

NCAA Championship

www.newsobserver.com/sports

NORTH CAROLINA 89, MICHIGAN STATE 72

NOT EVEN CLOSE

TAR HEELS COMPLETE DOMINANT TOURNAMENT TITLE RUN

UNC point guard Ty Lawson (5), who set an NCAA championship game record with eight steals, beats the Michigan State defense to the basket in scoring two of his game-high 21 points.
STAFF PHOTO BY CHUCK LIDDY

Goal reached in emphatic fashion

DETROIT – After North Carolina dashed past Michigan State and everyone else to the national basketball championship, the best description of the 2008-09 Tar Heels' superiority remained the words spoken by Brad Greenberg way back on March 18.

A day before Carolina began its six-game NCAA Tournament blitz, the Radford coach sat on a small stage in the Greensboro Coliseum and fished for precisely the correct words to explain his team's

Caulton

North Carolina sets records in building a 55-34 halftime lead, then holds off Michigan State to win its second NCAA Tournament in five seasons.

BY ROBBI PICKERAL
STAFF WRITER

DETROIT – As he went down the bench, alternately pumping his fist and hugging his teammates with a minute left Monday night, you could see it all in North Carolina forward Tyler Hansbrough's expression:

The elation. The relief. The redemption.

No matter the outcome of Monday's game, Hansbrough — one of the most decorated players in school history — would have left UNC a winner. But by helping shellac Michigan State 89-72 at Ford Field, he finished his career with the ultimate emotion: the pride of being a national champion.

"Sounds like I made a

Return engagement ends perfectly

BY KEN TYSIAC
STAFF WRITER

DETROIT – Bobby Frasor remembers hearing it from the moment Ty Lawson, Wayne Ellington and Danny Green announced on June 16 they were returning for the 2008-09 season instead of leaving for the NBA.

Tyler Hansbrough, the reigning national player of the year, already had made it clear he was coming back to a team that reached the NCAA semifinals. Now the entire starting lineup was returning.

Return engagement ends perfectly

North Carolina vs. [8]Michigan State // W 89-72   April 6, 2009

DETROIT — Bobby Frasor remembers hearing it from the moment Ty Lawson, Wayne Ellington and Danny Green announced on June 16 they were returning for the 2008-09 season instead of leaving for the NBA.

Tyler Hansbrough, the reigning national player of the year, already had made it clear he was coming back to a team that reached the NCAA semifinals. Now the entire starting lineup was returning.

The players understood what would be expected of them. Nothing less than a perfect season — an easy, perhaps unbeaten run to the national championship.

"There were articles written that day — 'Can they go perfect? Can they be UNLV?' Whatever," senior guard Frasor said.

The season wasn't perfect, but the ending was as the Tar Heels celebrated the school's fifth NCAA championship after defeating Michigan State on Monday night.

Perfection, a goal that existed briefly outside the program rather than within, had been dashed on the fourth day of January, when Boston College shocked North Carolina at Chapel Hill in its ACC opener. The Tar Heels entered the NCAA Tournament with four losses.

But in some ways, persevering through injuries and uncertainties made this trip to the NCAA final even more rewarding.

"It was difficult," Hansbrough said the day before the team left Chapel Hill for the Final Four. "We started off ACC play in kind of a tough position, and people started doubting us. We just stayed with each other as a team and listened to Coach, and started gradually improving, a little bit and a little bit. And here we are."

For coach Roy Williams, the pressure this season had nothing to do with fans, the media or even the defenses the Tar Heels faced.

His angst came out of heartfelt concern to do right by players who delayed professional careers to cast their lots with him. By the season opener on Nov. 12, Hansbrough was suffering from a stress reaction in his right shin.

Lawson suffered a jammed right big toe before the regular season finale against Duke. At the beginning of the season, Williams fretted over his practice routine. He cut short drills out of fear Hansbrough might hurt himself.

Williams agonized over the right time to bring Lawson back into the lineup. The junior point guard wound up missing three games but played against Duke after receiving a painkilling injection, a procedure an ashen-faced Williams later said would not be repeated when Lawson's injury lingered.

"Those are the things that I'm going to remember this season for, the adversity with the injuries," Williams said.

No injury affected the team as much as the fracture in wing Marcus Ginyard's left foot. Players were out together in Chapel Hill one night when Ginyard grabbed Danny Green's cell phone.

Ginyard wanted his fellow seniors to be the first ones to know his plans to sit out the rest of the season. To prevent the rest of the team from finding out, Ginyard thumbed a message to Green on the cell phone screen.

"I was in shock," Green said. "I was like, 'What? You're doing what?' "

Ginyard, the team's best defensive player and emotional leader, had become convinced he couldn't help the team this season. He was going to redshirt, which meant he wouldn't leave the program with the seniors who joined him in one of the nation's top recruiting classes in 2005.

THAT WINNING FEELING

THE TAR HEELS ENJOYED THE RIDE ON THE WAY TO THE 2009 NCAA CHAMPIONSHIP

Tyler Hansbrough savors North Carolina's national championship after the Tar Heels' dominating, 89-72 victory over Michigan State on Monday night in Detroit.
STAFF PHOTO BY CHUCK LIDDY

On Feb. 3, the same night that Ginyard made his decision public, Williams announced that reserve guard William Graves was suspended for the rest of the season.

With freshman center Tyler Zeller also out with a broken left wrist, the Tar Heels' vaunted depth had all but evaporated. ∎

— Ken Tysiac

OPPOSITE LEFT: North Carolina's Ty Lawson (5) shoots for two points in the first half against Michigan State defenders. CHUCK LIDDY/THE NEWS & OBSERVER

OPPOSITE RIGHT: Michigan State's Goran Suton (14) has to move the ball outside against North Carolina's Wayne Ellington (22) and Ed Davis (32). ROBERT WILLETT/THE NEWS & OBSERVER

PREVIOUS TOP: North Carolina's Deon Thompson (21) reacts after making a shot and being fouled in the first half. ROBERT WILLETT/THE NEWS & OBSERVER

PREVIOUS BOTTOM: Coach Roy Williams reacts to a call after catching a loose ball in the first half of play against Michigan State. ROBERT WILLETT/ THE NEWS & OBSERVER

PREVIOUS RIGHT: North Carolina's Deon Thompson (21) rips a rebound. ROBERT WILLETT/THE NEWS & OBSERVER

FOLLOWING LEFT: North Carolina's Ty Lawson (5) races between Michigan State's Travis Walton (5) and Raymar Morgan (2) in the second half. ROBERT WILLETT/THE NEWS & OBSERVER

FOLLOWING RIGHT: North Carolina's Deon Thompson (21) shoots over the defense of Michigan State's Delvon Roe (10) in the first half. CHUCK LIDDY/ THE NEWS & OBSERVER

Heels fulfill their destiny; Season of ups and downs ends with college basketball's highest achievement

North Carolina vs. ⁸Michigan State // W 89-72   April 6, 2009

At North Carolina, basketball has long been about winning championships, clipping nets, hoisting trophies and hanging banners.

So Monday night at Detroit's Ford Field, in a memorable Motown moment, the Tar Heels again reached the pinnacle, claiming their second national championship in five seasons.

This veteran team — energized by ACC Player of the Year Ty Lawson, empowered by four-time All-American Tyler Hansbrough and guided by Hall of Fame coach Roy Williams — completed a season-long mission after losing to Kansas in a semifinal debacle last April.

The nitpickers once pointed at his teams' losses on the biggest stage. The Hall of Fame coach has led seven teams to the Final Four, including three in six seasons since leaving Kansas for UNC after the 2002-03 season. After leading the Tar Heels to their second title in five seasons, who's left to find fault? Though the team was picked an early favorite, the 2008-09 season was anything but easy. Injuries had Williams shuffling his lineup, and he shrugged off an 0-2 start in the ACC to clinch the regular-season title. Rolling in March, the Tar Heels beat their first five NCAA opponents by double figures.

With a sharp focus and a resolve that matched their talent, these Tar Heels overcame injuries, a shaky ACC start and 30 opponents to equal the No. 1 preseason ranking.

Lawson set the tempo during the championship run after overcoming perhaps the most publicized toe injury since Dr. James Naismith hung the first peach basket.

Hansbrough, the ACC's all-time leading scorer, completed his record-filled resume in Detroit with help from starters Lawson, Wayne Ellington, Danny Green and Deon Thompson, standout freshman reserve Ed Davis and backup guard Bobby Frasor.

"It was one of the big factors why I came back," Hansbrough said before the Final Four.

After last season, Lawson, Green and Ellington tested their NBA draft prospects, creating a cloud of concern among Tar Heel loyalists. Their decision to return and join Hansbrough for his final year sent expectations spiraling into the stratosphere.

The hoopla began in the summer, starting with casual basketball banter, then escalated into bold forecasts that this North Carolina team could produce a perfect season.

Williams tried to put a muzzle on such media hype. Turns out, the Tar Heels weren't impeccable (four losses), just powerful.

After North Carolina started with 13 straight victories, all by decisive margins, loquacious Green suggested the Heels could benefit from a "tough" game.

They got it.

Boston College stunned Carolina 85-78 on Jan. 4 in Chapel Hill, where Tyrese Rice outplayed Lawson. A week later in Winston-Salem, Wake Forest gave UNC a shocking 0-2 ACC start with a 92-89 win in which Jeff Teague overshadowed Lawson.

Vulnerable against penetrating guards, the Tar Heels needed their perimeter defensive stopper. But Marcus Ginyard was injured and eventually was granted a medical redshirt season.

Promising freshman Tyler Zeller also ended up with an injury. Lawson was catching criticism. Skeptics even questioned Hansbrough's durability as he worked to overcome a preseason shin problem.

The team's depth was diminishing, and the defense had some cracks. Yet after the defeat at Wake Forest, Carolina regained its winning way, losing only twice more — at Maryland in a regular-season spectacle and then to Florida State in the ACC Tournament, when Lawson was sidelined with his big toe injury.

That ACC Tournament loss, coupled with Lawson's return in the NCAA regionals, fueled Carolina's return to normalcy.

The Tar Heels drove to the Final Four in cruise-control style, winning the first four games handily.

Ellington unleashed his artful shooting stroke. Green rediscovered his touch. Lawson provided the fast tempo Williams prefers, and the team defense locked down with more tenacity and consistency.

Once in Detroit, the Tar Heels wouldn't be denied. Not this time, not after the 2008 misadventure in San Antonio.

In the end, when the games mattered the most, no team was finer than North Carolina. ∎

— A.J. Carr

RIGHT: North Carolina's Tyler Hansbrough (50) shoots a first-half foul shot against Michigan State.
CHUCK LIDDY/THE NEWS & OBSERVER

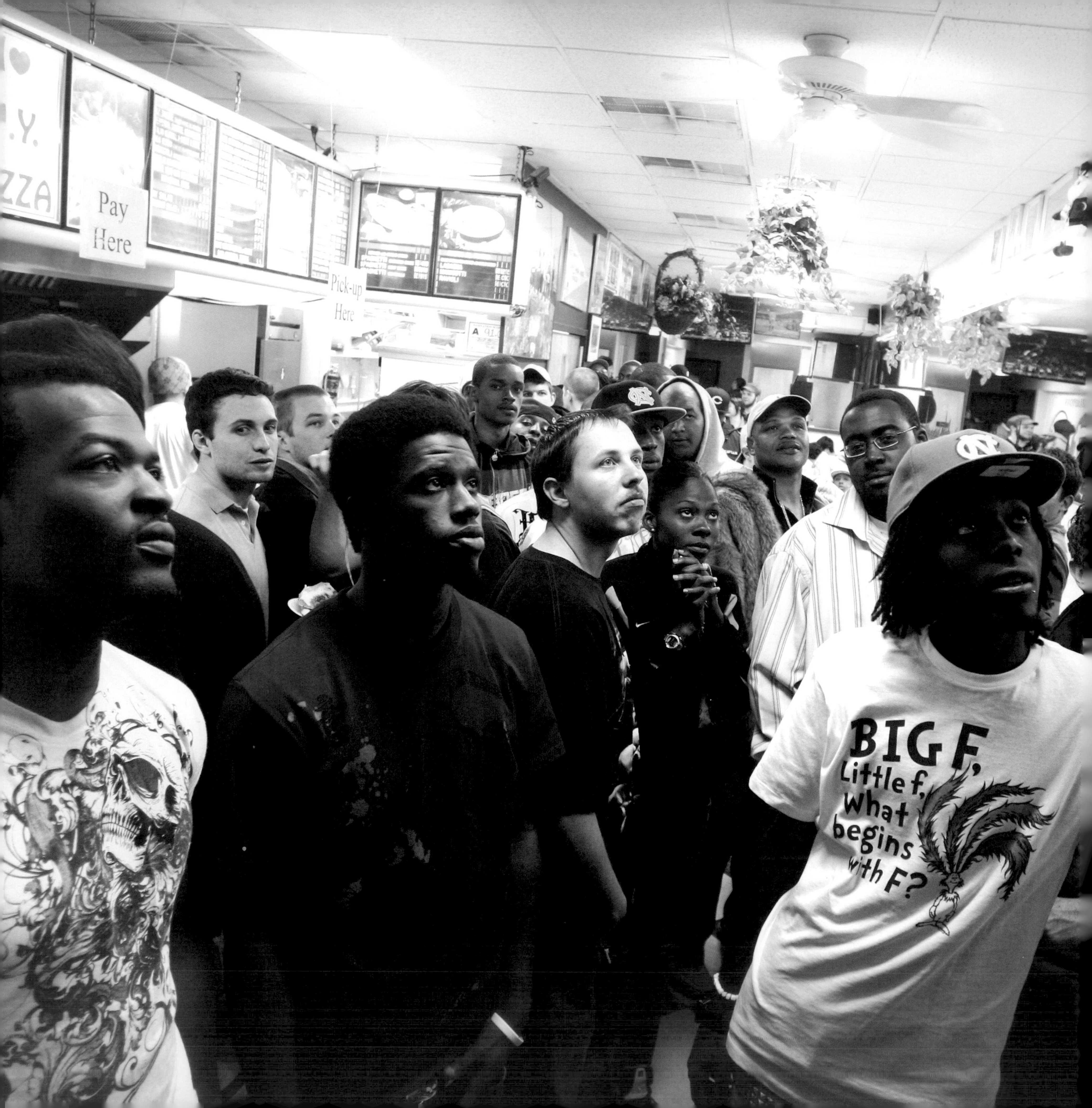
Pay
Here
Pick-up
Here
BIG F,
Little f,
What
begins
with F?

NORTH CAROLINA TAR HEELS

2009 NATIONAL CHAMPIONS • UNC 89, MICHIGAN STATE 72

GIMME FIVE

TAR HEELS CAPTURE THEIR FIFTH NCAA CHAMPIONSHIP

Senior Danny Green and his Tar Heels teammates show off the NCAA Division I men's basketball trophy, with a little help from coach Roy Williams, on Monday night in Detroit.
STAFF PHOTO BY ROBERT WILLETT

LEFT: UNC's Patrick Moody (35) and his teammates celebrate the Tar Heels' 89-72 victory over Michigan State as time expires. ROBERT WILLETT/ THE NEWS & OBSERVER

PREVIOUS LEFT: Fans, including Josh Edwards, left, Rashawn Seymore, center, and Kevone Best, watch the second half action at I Love N.Y. Pizza in Chapel Hill. ETHAN HYMAN/THE NEWS & OBSERVER

PREVIOUS TOP: Kate Tweedy, a UNC graduate student, cheers on the Tar Heels while watching UNC's game against Michigan State at the Dean E. Smith Center in Chapel Hill. Laura Vidales, a UNC graduate, is to the left. ETHAN HYMAN/THE NEWS & OBSERVER

PREVIOUS BOTTOM: Thousands of fans cheer on the Tar Heels while watching UNC's game at the Dean E. Smith Center. ETHAN HYMAN/THE NEWS & OBSERVER

131

ABOVE: UNC's Wayne Ellington (22), the MVP, weeps as the Tar Heels celebrate their victory over Michigan State. ROBERT WILLETT/THE NEWS & OBSERVER

TOP: UNC's Tyler Hansbrough (50) embraces Marcus Ginyard as the Tar Heels celebrate. ROBERT WILLETT/ THE NEWS & OBSERVER

RIGHT: UNC's Tyler Hansbrough (50) celebrates the Tar Heels victory over Michigan State. ROBERT WILLETT/ THE NEWS & OBSERVER

OPPOSITE: The Tar Heels celebrate their victory over Michigan State. ROBERT WILLETT/THE NEWS & OBSERVER

PREVIOUS LEFT: UNC coach Roy Williams celebrates after winning the 2009 NCAA Championship. ROBERT WILLETT/THE NEWS & OBSERVER

PREVIOUS MIDDLE: UNC's Deon Thompson (21) and his teammates celebrate the Tar Heels' victory. ROBERT WILLETT/THE NEWS & OBSERVER

PREVIOUS RIGHT: UNC senior J.B. Tanner (15) and his teammates celebrate the Tar Heels' victory. ROBERT WILLETT/THE NEWS & OBSERVER

ABOVE: North Carolina head coach Roy Williams cuts down the nets at Ford Field. CHUCK LIDDY/THE NEWS & OBSERVER

TOP: North Carolina's Ty Lawson (5) cuts down the nets. CHUCK LIDDY/THE NEWS & OBSERVER

LEFT: UNC coach Roy Williams holds a net as he and his players watch the "One Shining Moment" video after defeating Michigan State. ROBERT WILLETT/THE NEWS & OBSERVER

ABOVE: Franklin Street in Chapel Hill erupts as thousands of Tar Heel fans celebrate UNC's victory over Michigan State. SHAWN ROCCO/THE NEWS & OBSERVER

OPPOSITE LEFT: Coach Roy Williams thanks Tar Heel fans as the team takes center stage at the Dean E. Smith Center the day after winning the 2009 NCAA men's basketball title. SHAWN ROCCO/THE NEWS & OBSERVER

OPPOSITE RIGHT: An estimated 13,000 UNC students and fans gathered for the celebration. SHAWN ROCCO/THE NEWS & OBSERVER

FOLLOWING LEFT: Roy Williams talks to the crowd during a welcome home celebration for the Tar Heels on Tuesday, April 7, 2009. ETHAN HYMAN/THE NEWS & OBSERVER

FOLLOWING RIGHT: UNC senior Mike Copeland speaks at the welcome home celebration. ETHAN HYMAN/THE NEWS & OBSERVER

FOLLOWING BOTTOM: The team and fans embrace in typical Tar Heel fashion as the pep band plays the school's alma mater, "Hark the Sound," at the welcome home celebration. SHAWN ROCCO/THE NEWS & OBSERVER

Game Log

Date	Opponent	Result	Record (conf.)
REGULAR SEASON			
November 15, 2008	Pennsylvania	W 86-71	1-0
November 18, 2008	Kentucky	W 77-58	2-0
November 21, 2008	at UC Santa Barbara	W 84-67	3-0
November 24, 2008	at Chaminade	W 115-70	4-0
November 25, 2008	at Oregon	W 98-69	5-0
November 26, 2008	No. 9 Notre Dame	W 102-87	6-0
November 30, 2008	North Carolina-Asheville	W 116-48	7-0
December 3, 2008	No. 13 Michigan State	W 98-63	8-0
December 13, 2008	Oral Roberts	W 100-84	9-0
December 18, 2008	Evansville	W 91-73	10-0
December 20, 2008	Valparaiso	W 85-63	11-0
December 28, 2008	Rutgers	W 97-75	12-0
December 31, 2008	at Nevada	W 84-61	13-0
January 4, 2009	Boston College	L 85-78	13-1 (0-1)
January 7, 2009	C of Charleston	W 108-70	14-1
January 11, 2009	at No. 4 Wake Forest	L 92-89	14-2 (0-2)
January 15, 2009	at Virginia	W 83-61	15-2 (1-2)
January 17, 2009	Miami (FL)	W 82-65	16-2 (2-2)
January 21, 2009	No. 10 Clemson	W 94-70	17-2 (3-2)
January 28, 2009	at Florida State	W 80-77	18-2 (4-2)
January 31, 2009	at North Carolina State	W 93-76	19-2 (5-2)
February 3, 2009	Maryland	W 108-91	20-2 (6-2)
February 7, 2009	Virginia	W 76-61	21-2 (7-2)
February 11, 2009	at No. 6 Duke	W 101-87	22-2 (8-2)
February 15, 2009	at Miami (FL)	W 69-65	23-2 (9-2)
February 18, 2009	North Carolina State	W 89-80	24-2 (10-2)
February 21, 2009	at Maryland	L 88-85	24-3 (10-3)
February 28, 2009	Georgia Tech	W 104-74	25-3 (11-3)
March 4, 2009	at Virginia Tech	W 86-78	26-3 (12-3)
March 8, 2009	No. 7 Duke	W 79-71	27-3 (13-3)
ACC TOURNAMENT			
March 13, 2009	Virginia Tech	W 79-76	28-3
March 14, 2009	No. 16 Florida State	L 73-70	28-4
NCAA TOURNAMENT			
March 19, 2009	Radford	W 101-58	29-4
March 21, 2009	No. 21 LSU	W 84-70	30-4
March 27, 2009	No. 10 Gonzaga	W 98-77	31-4
March 29, 2009	No. 7 Oklahoma	W 72-60	32-4
April 4, 2009	No. 11 Villanova	W 83-69	33-4
April 6, 2009	No. 8 Michigan State	W 89-72	34-4

First Round	Second Round	Regionals	National Semifinals

Louisville **1**

Louisville (74-54)

Dayton

*Morehead St. **16**

Louisville (79-72)

Ohio St. **8**

Siena (74-72 2OT)

Siena **9**

Utah **5**

Louisville (103-64)

Arizona (84-71)

Miami

Arizona **12**

Wake Forest **4**

Arizona (71-57)

Cleveland St. (84-69)

Cleveland St. **13**

Michigan St. (64-52)

Midwest Regional
Indianapolis

West Virginia **6**

Dayton (68-60)

Minneapolis

Dayton **11**

Kansas (60-43)

Kansas **3**

Kansas (84-74)

North Dakota St. **14**

Boston College **7**

Michigan St. (67-62)

Southern California (72-55)

Minneapolis

Southern California **10**

Michigan St. **2**

Michigan St. (74-69)

Michigan St. (77-62)

Robert Morris **15**

Connecticut **1**

Connecticut (103-47)

Philadelphia

Chattanooga **16**

Connecticut (92-66)

Detroit

BYU **8**

Texas A&M (79-66)

Texas A&M **9**

Purdue **5**

Connecticut (72-60)

Michigan State

Purdue (61-56)

Portland

UNI **12**

Washington **4**

Purdue (76-74)

Washington (71-58)

Mississippi St. **13**

West Regional
Glendale

Connecticut (82-75)

Marquette **6**

Marquette (58-57)

Boise

Utah St. **11**

Missouri (83-79)

Missouri **3**

Missouri (78-59)

Cornell **14**

California **7**

Missouri (102-91)

Maryland (84-71)

Kansas City

Maryland **10**

Memphis **2**

Memphis (89-70)

Memphis (81-70)

Cal St. Northridge **15**

North Carolina

NATIONAL CHAMPIONS

National Semifinals	Regionals	Second Round	First Round	

National Semifinals

Regionals

Second Round

First Round

		1 Pittsburgh
	Pittsburgh (72-62)	
Pittsburgh (84-76)		**16** East Tenn. St.
		8 Oklahoma St.
	Oklahoma St. (77-75)	
Pittsburgh (60-55)		**9** Tennessee
		5 Florida St.
	Wisconsin (61-59 OT)	
Xavier (60-49)		**12** Wisconsin
		4 Xavier
	Xavier (77-59)	
		13 Portland St.

Dayton

Boise

Villanova (78-76)

**East Regional
Boston**

		6 UCLA
	UCLA (65-64)	
Villanova (89-69)		**11** VCU
		3 Villanova
	Villanova (80-67)	
Villanova (77-54)		**14** American
		7 Texas
	Texas (76-62)	
Duke (74-69)		**10** Minnesota
		2 Duke
	Duke (86-62)	
		15 Binghamton

Philadelphia

Greensboro

Detroit

North Carolina

		1 North Carolina
	North Carolina (101-58)	
North Carolina (84-70)		**16** Radford
		8 LSU
	LSU (75-71)	
North Carolina (98-77)		**9** Butler
		5 Illinois
	Western Ky. (76-72)	
Gonzaga (83-81)		**12** Western Ky.
		4 Gonzaga
	Gonzaga (77-64)	
		13 Akron

Greensboro

Portland

North Carolina (72-60)

**South Regional
Memphis**

		6 Arizona St.
	Arizona St. (66-57)	
Syracuse (78-67)		**11** Temple
		3 Syracuse
	Syracuse (59-44)	
Oklahoma (84-71)		**14** Stephen F. Austin
		7 Clemson
	Michigan (62-59)	
Oklahoma (73-63)		**10** Michigan
		2 Oklahoma
	Oklahoma (82-54)	
		15 Morgan St.

Miami

Kansas City

Season Stats

NAME	GM	MIN	PTS	PTSTOT	FG%	FT%	3P%	REB	REBTOT	AST	ASTTOT	TO	STL	STLTOT	BLK	BLKTOT	PF
Bobby Frasor	38	17.4	2.6	100	0.333	0.462	0.274	2	75	1.4	54	0.7	0.6	22	0.1	5	1.4
Danny Green	38	27.4	13.1	497	0.471	0.852	0.418	4.7	178	2.7	104	1.7	1.8	67	1.3	51	2.2
Deon Thompson	38	24.8	10.6	401	0.492	0.646	0	5.7	216	0.7	26	1.3	0.9	35	1.1	40	2.2
Ed Davis	38	18.8	6.7	253	0.518	0.573	0	6.6	250	0.6	22	1.1	0.4	14	1.7	65	1.9
J.B. Tanner	21	2.1	1.1	23	0.421	0.333	0.357	0.3	7	0	1	0	0	1	0	0	0.2
Jack Wooten	19	1.9	0.5	10	0.364	0.25	0.2	0.3	5	0.1	2	0.1	0	0	0	0	0.1
Justin Watts	27	3.1	0.7	19	0.242	0.429	0	0.7	20	0.2	5	0.3	0.1	2	0.1	3	0.2
Larry Drew II	38	9.6	1.4	53	0.351	0.412	0.231	1.1	41	1.9	74	1.2	0.4	15	0	1	0.9
Marc Campbell	20	1.9	0.2	4	0.333	1	0	0.3	5	0.5	9	0.4	0.1	2	0	0	0.1
Marcus Ginyard	3	12.3	1.3	4	0.25	0.5	0	2.7	8	1.3	4	1	0.7	2	0	0	1.7
Mike Copeland	17	2.5	0.8	13	0.25	1	0	0.8	13	0.1	1	0.1	0	0	0	0	0.5
Patrick Moody	21	2.1	1	22	0.583	0.615	0	0.7	15	0	0	0.1	0.1	2	0.1	3	0.3
Ty Lawson	35	29.9	16.6	581	0.532	0.798	0.472	3	104	6.6	230	1.9	2.1	75	0.1	5	1.7
Tyler Hansbrough	34	30.3	20.7	704	0.514	0.841	0.391	8.1	276	1	34	1.9	1.2	42	0.4	12	2.3
Tyler Zeller	15	7.8	3.1	47	0.472	0.765	0	2	30	0.2	3	0.5	0.2	3	0.2	3	1.3
Wayne Ellington	38	30.4	15.8	602	0.483	0.777	0.417	4.9	186	2.7	101	1.6	0.9	36	0.2	6	1.5
Will Graves	20	11.2	4	80	0.437	0.889	0.278	2.6	51	0.8	15	1.2	0.4	7	0.1	2	1.6

ACC Team Stats

TEAM	GM	PTS	PTSTOT	FG%	FT%	3P%	REB	REBTOT	AST	ASTTOT	TO	STL	STLTOT	BLK	BLKTOT	PF
Boston College	33	74.9	2473	0.446	0.734	0.337	37.2	1229	14.8	490	13.4	6.2	203	4.4	144	18
Clemson	31	79	2448	0.467	0.684	0.379	36.9	1145	15	464	14.4	9.4	290	5.8	180	17.9
Duke	34	78	2653	0.448	0.723	0.349	36.6	1245	13.4	455	12.3	8.5	289	4.1	139	18
Florida State	34	68.6	2333	0.435	0.723	0.343	35.9	1220	12.3	417	15.7	8.2	278	5.8	198	18.8
Georgia Tech	31	71.2	2208	0.436	0.63	0.323	39.1	1211	14.9	462	16.8	8.3	256	5	154	19.6
Maryland	33	71.5	2358	0.422	0.768	0.331	36.7	1211	14.7	484	12.5	7.7	255	4.3	141	16.6
Miami (FL)	30	72.9	2187	0.428	0.679	0.371	40.1	1203	12.6	379	13.2	6	180	3.9	116	16.7
North Carolina	32	90.2	2886	0.48	0.761	0.376	42.3	1354	18.4	590	12.8	8.5	271	5.3	171	15.9
North Carolina State	30	73	2189	0.475	0.717	0.375	35.8	1075	15.3	458	14.5	5.6	168	3.8	114	16
Virginia	28	70	1960	0.417	0.742	0.316	36.8	1030	12.4	348	14.8	6.4	179	4	112	18.9
Virginia Tech	32	71.5	2288	0.436	0.72	0.34	37.3	1193	13.1	418	13.7	6.4	206	4.6	147	18.4
Wake Forest	30	81.4	2441	0.489	0.712	0.318	41	1229	13.2	395	15.8	8.5	254	5.4	163	18.8

Legend: **GM** - Games played. **MIN** - Minutes average. **PTS** - Points average. **PTSTOT** - Points total. **FG%** - Field goal percentage. **FT%** - Free throw percentage. **3P%** - Three point percentage. **REB** - Rebounds average. **REBTOT** - Rebounds total. **AST** - Assists average. **ASTTOT** - Assists total. **TO** - Turnovers average. **STL** - Steals average. **STLTOT** - Steals total. **BLK** - Blocks average. **BLKTOT** - Blocks total. **PF** - Personal fouls average.